Oxford First Dictionary

Compiled by Evelyn Goldsmith, Andrew Delahunty
Illustrated by Bernice Lum
Literacy Consultant Kate Ruttle

OXFORD
UNIVERSITY PRESS

OXFORD
UNIVERSITY PRESS

Great Clarendon Street, Oxford OX2 6DP

Oxford University Press is a department of the University of Oxford.
It furthers the University's objective of excellence in research, scholarship,
and education by publishing worldwide in

Oxford   New York

Auckland   Cape Town   Dar es Salaam   Hong Kong   Karachi
Kuala Lumpur   Madrid   Melbourne   Mexico City   Nairobi
New Delhi   Shanghai   Taipei   Toronto

With offices in

Argentina   Austria   Brazil   Chile   Czech Republic   France   Greece
Guatemala   Hungary   Italy   Japan   Poland   Portugal   Singapore
South Korea   Switzerland   Thailand   Turkey   Ukraine   Vietnam

First published in 1993 as My First Oxford Dictionary
Second edition 1997
First published in 2002 as Oxford First Dictionary
Second edition 2007

British Library Cataloguing in Publication Data

Data available

ISBN 978-0-19-911519-8 hardback
ISBN 978-0-19-911520-4 paperback

7 9 10 8 6

Printed in Singapore by KHL Printing Co. Pte Ltd.

www.schooldictionaries.co.uk

Introduction

The **Oxford First Dictionary** is a lively, colourful dictionary for children aged five years upwards. The selection of entries is based on extensive classroom research into words young children come across in their reading and use in their writing and speaking. Younger readers will use this dictionary to see how familiar words are spelt, while more confident readers will look up a word for its meaning.

cuddle verb

introduces simple grammar such as word classes like verbs or nouns

cuddles, cuddling, cuddled

some word classes change their endings depending on their tense

younger children enjoy matching the illustrations to the definition; older readers find the illustrations help them tackle new words and support their understanding of the written definitions

cup noun **cups**

introduces plurals

early adjective **earlier, earliest**

some words have comparative and superlative forms

fresh adjective **fresher, freshest**
1 Fresh food has just been picked or made.
2 Fresh water is not salty.
3 Fresh air is clean and pure.

words can have more than one meaning

fly ❶ verb **flies, flying, flew, flown**
1 When something flies, it moves through the air.
2 When people fly, they travel in an aircraft.
We are flying to Dublin tomorrow.

the same word can be used in quite different ways

fly ❷ noun **flies**
A fly is a small insect with one pair of wings.

Use the special picture section to become a **Word Explorer!**

- Spelling success
- Punctuation
- Words we use too much
- Opposites
- Place and position words

- More than one
- Time, days, months and seasons
- Colours and shapes
- Your body
- Words we use a lot

above
Above means higher up. *Yasmin painted a yellow sun above the house.*

accident noun accidents
An accident is something nasty that was not meant to happen. *He broke his arm in a car accident.*

ache verb aches, aching, ached
If part of your body aches, it keeps on hurting.

act verb acts, acting, acted
If you act, you pretend to be someone else in a play, show, or film.

add verb adds, adding, added
1 When you add something, you put it with something else. *Mix the eggs and sugar. Then add flour.*
2 When you add numbers, you work out how many you get when you put them together. *Three add two equals five.*

$$3+2=5$$

address noun addresses
Someone's address is the number of their house, and the name of the street and town where they live.

adult noun adults
An adult is a person or animal that has grown up.

adventure noun adventures
An adventure is something exciting that happens to you.

aeroplane noun aeroplanes
An aeroplane is a flying machine with wings, and usually one or more engines.

afraid adjective
Someone who is afraid thinks something bad might happen to them. *Sarah is afraid of the dark.*

afternoon noun afternoons
The afternoon is the time from the middle of the day until about six o'clock.

against
If you are against somebody, you are on the opposite side to them. *We played a game of football, children against grown-ups.*

age noun
The age of someone or something is how old they are.

agree verb **agrees, agreeing, agreed**
If you agree with someone, you think the same as they do.

air noun
Air is what everyone breathes. It is made of gases that we cannot see.

airport noun **airports**
An airport is a place where aeroplanes land and take off.

alive adjective
A person, animal, or plant that is alive is living at the moment.

allow verb **allows, allowing, allowed**
If someone allows you to do something, they let you do it. *Dogs are not allowed to come in the shop.*

almost
Almost means very nearly. *We almost missed the bus.*

alone adjective
If someone is alone, there is nobody with them. *Our cat has been alone in the house all day.*

alphabet noun **alphabets**
The alphabet is all the letters that are used in writing, arranged in a special order.

also
Also means as well. *I have a pet rabbit and also two hamsters.*

always
If something always happens, it happens every time.

ambulance noun **ambulances**
An ambulance is a special van for taking people to hospital when they are ill or badly hurt.

amphibian noun **amphibians**
Amphibians are animals that start their lives in water and later change so they are able to live on land. Frogs and toads are amphibians.

ancient adjective
Things that are ancient are very old.

angry adjective **angrier, angriest**
If you are angry, you are not pleased at all with what someone has done or said.

animal noun **animals**
An animal is something that lives, can move about, and is not a plant. Elephants, parrots, bees, goldfish, and people are all animals.

ankle noun **ankles**
Your ankle is the part of your body where your leg joins your foot.

a
b
c
d
e
f
g
h
i
j
k
l
m
n
o
p
q
r
s
t
u
v
w
x
y
z

5

annoy verb **annoys, annoying, annoyed**
If someone annoys you, they make you angry.

answer verb **answers, answering, answered**
When you answer, you speak when someone calls you or asks you a question. *'Is anybody there?', asked Hollie, but nobody answered.*

ant noun **ants**
An ant is a tiny insect. Ants live in large groups.

ape noun **apes**
An ape is an animal like a large monkey without a tail. Chimpanzees and gorillas are apes.

appear verb **appears, appearing, appeared**
If something appears, you can suddenly see it. *The clouds parted and the moon appeared.*

apple noun **apples**
An apple is a round, crisp fruit. Apples have green, red, or yellow skins.

apron noun **aprons**
An apron is a piece of clothing that you wear over your other clothes to keep them clean when you are cooking or painting.

area noun **areas**
An area is part of a town or place. *We live in a nice area next to the park.*

argue verb **argues, arguing, argued**
When you argue with somebody, you talk about things you do not agree on. *My brother and I are always arguing.*

arm noun **arms**
Your arm is the part of your body between your shoulder and your hand.

armchair noun **armchairs**
An armchair is a comfortable chair with parts at the side to rest your arms on.

army noun **armies**
An army is a large group of soldiers who are trained to fight on land in a war.

arrange verb **arranges, arranging, arranged**
If you arrange things, you put them in order.

arrow noun **arrows**
An arrow is a pointed stick that you shoot from a bow.

art noun
Art is something special that someone has made, like a drawing, painting, or carving.

ask verb **asks, asking, asked**
1 When you ask a question, you are trying to find something out. *'What is your name?' Tommy asked.*
2 If you ask for something, you say you want it to be given to you. *'Can I have some chocolate?' Rachel asked.*

asleep adjective
When you are asleep, you are resting completely, with your eyes closed, and you don't know what is going on around you.

astronaut noun **astronauts**
An astronaut is a person who travels in space.

ate See **eat**.
My sister ate too much at the party.

attack verb **attacks, attacking, attacked**
If you attack someone, you try to hurt them.

attention noun
When you pay attention to somebody, you listen carefully and think about what they are saying.

audience noun **audiences**
An audience is a group of people who have come to a place to watch or listen to something.

aunt noun **aunts**
Your aunt is the sister of your mother or father, or the wife of your uncle.

author noun **authors**
An author is a person who writes a book or story.

autumn noun **autumns**
Autumn is the part of the year when it gets colder, and leaves fall from the trees.

awake adjective
When you are awake, you are not asleep.

a
b
c
d
e
f
g
h
i
j
k
l
m
n
o
p
q
r
s
t
u
v
w
x
y
z

a
b
c
d
e
f
g
h
i
j
k
l
m
n
o
p
q
r
s
t
u
v
w
x
y
z

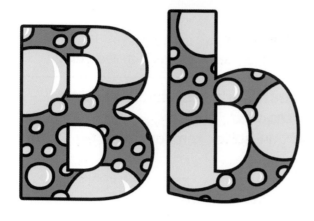

baby noun **babies**
A baby is a very young child.

back noun **backs**
1 The back of something is the part opposite the front. *Dan sat at the back of the boat.*
2 Your back is the back part of your body.

bad adjective **worse, worst**
1 Things that are bad are not good. *Sugar is bad for your teeth.*
2 Bad food is not fit to eat.

bag noun **bags**
A bag is used to hold or carry things.

bake verb **bakes, baking, baked**
When you bake something, you cook it in an oven.

balance verb **balances, balancing, balanced**
When you balance something, you keep it steady. *Can you balance a ball on your head?*

ball noun **balls**
A ball is a round object that is used in games.

balloon noun **balloons**
A balloon is a rubber bag that you can blow into and make bigger.

banana noun **bananas**
A banana is a long, curved fruit with a thick, yellow skin.

band noun **bands**
1 A band is a group of people who play musical instruments together.
2 A band can also be a strip of material round something.

bank noun **banks**
1 A bank is the ground along the side of a river or canal.
2 A bank is also a place that looks after money for people.

bar noun **bars**
A bar is a long, thin piece of wood or metal. *The monkey put its hand through the bars of its cage.*

bare adjective **barer, barest**
1 If part of someone's body is bare, it is not covered with anything. *Jenny was dancing in her bare feet.*
2 A room or cupboard that is bare has nothing in it.

bark ❶ noun
Bark is the hard covering round the trunk and branches of a tree.

bark ❷ verb **barks, barking, barked**
When dogs bark, they make a sudden, loud sound.

barn noun **barns**
A barn is a large building on a farm, where a farmer stores things like hay. Animals are sometimes kept in barns.

basket noun **baskets**
A basket is for holding or carrying things. Baskets are made of strips of material like straw or thin wood.

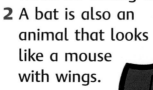

bat noun **bats**
1 A bat is a piece of wood for hitting the ball in a game.
2 A bat is also an animal that looks like a mouse with wings.

bath noun **baths**
A bath can be filled with water so that you can sit in it and wash yourself.

bathroom noun **bathrooms**
A bathroom is a room with a bath or shower.

battery noun **batteries**
A battery has electricity inside it. You put batteries in things like torches, watches, and radios to make them work.

beach noun **beaches**
A beach is land by the edge of the sea. It is usually covered with sand or small stones.

beak noun **beaks**
A beak is the hard part of a bird's mouth.

bear noun **bears**
A bear is a big, heavy animal with thick fur and sharp claws.

beard noun **beards**
A beard is the hair that grows on a man's chin and cheeks.

beat verb **beats, beating, beat, beaten**
1 If you beat someone in a race or game, you do better than them and win it.
2 To beat can also mean to keep hitting with a stick. *Don't let him beat the donkey.*

a
b
c
d
e
f
g
h
i
j
k
l
m
n
o
p
q
r
s
t
u
v
w
x
y
z

a
b
c
d
e
f
g
h
i
j
k
l
m
n
o
p
q
r
s
t
u
v
w
x
y
z

beautiful adjective
You say something is beautiful if you enjoy looking at it or listening to it. *What a beautiful painting!*

bed noun **beds**
A bed is a piece of furniture you sleep on.

bedroom noun **bedrooms**
A bedroom is a room you sleep in.

bee noun **bees**
A bee is an insect with wings. Bees make honey.

beetle noun **beetles**
A beetle is an insect with hard wing-covers.

before
Before means at an earlier time. *I brush my teeth before I go to bed.*

began See **begin**.
Tom began to read when he was four.

begin verb **begins, beginning, began, begun**
When you begin, you start something. *Begin running when I blow the whistle.*

begun See **begin**.
I have just begun a new drawing.

behave verb **behaves, behaving, behaved**
If someone tells you to behave, they want you to be good.

behind
Behind means at the back of something. *David hid behind a chair.*

believe verb **believes, believing, believed**
If you believe something, you feel that it is true. *Do you believe in ghosts?*

bell noun **bells**
A bell is a piece of metal that makes a ringing sound when you hit or shake it.

belong verb **belongs, belonging, belonged**
1 If something belongs to you, it is yours. *That pen belongs to me.*
2 If something belongs somewhere, that is its proper place. *Where do these plates belong?*

below
Below means lower down. *I sleep on the top bunk and my brother sleeps below.*

belt noun **belts**
A belt is a band you wear round your waist.

bench noun **benches**
A bench is a long seat for more than one person.

bend verb **bends, bending, bent**
If you bend something, you change its shape so it is no longer straight. *If Tom bends his knees he can touch his toes.*

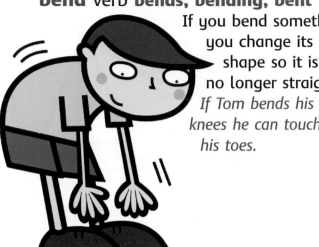

bent See **bend**.
I bent the piece of wire into a circle.

best adjective
Something or somebody that is best is better than any of the others. *Jamie is the best player in the team.*

better
1 If someone can do something better than you, they do it with more skill than you do. *Mum can draw better than Dad can.*
2 If one thing is better than another, it is more useful, or nearer to what you want. *Your red coat would be better today – it's warmer.*
3 If you are feeling better, you are well again. *I had a bad cough last week, but I'm better now.*

bicycle noun **bicycles**
A bicycle is a machine that you can ride. Bicycles have two wheels and pedals which you turn with your feet.

big adjective **bigger, biggest**
Somebody or something big is large. *An elephant is much bigger than a mouse.*

bin noun **bins**
A bin is something to put things in. You can use bins to store things like bread or flour. Some bins are for rubbish.

bird noun **birds**
A bird is an animal that has wings, feathers, and a beak. Most birds can fly.

birthday noun **birthdays**
Your birthday is the day you were born. *My birthday is on the 24th of November.*

biscuit noun **biscuits**
A biscuit is a kind of small, thin, dry cake.

bit ❶ See **bite**.
Sam bit into the apple.

bit ❷ noun **bits**
A bit is a tiny piece of something.

bite verb **bites, biting, bit, bitten**
If you bite something, you use your teeth to cut into it.

bitten See **bite**.
The parrot has bitten my finger.

a b c d e f g h i j k l m n o p q r s t u v w x y z

blame verb **blames, blaming, blamed**
If you blame someone, you think it is because of them that something bad has happened. *Mum always blames me if the room gets messy.*

blanket noun **blankets**
A blanket is a thick cover for a bed.

blew See **blow**.
Kerry blew out the candles on her birthday cake.

blind adjective
Someone who is blind cannot see at all.

block noun **blocks**
A block is a thick piece of something solid like wood or stone.

blood noun
Blood is the red liquid that moves round inside your body.

blow verb **blows, blowing, blew, blown**
1 When you blow, you make air come out of your mouth. *See if you can blow the candles out.*
2 When the wind blows, it moves the air. *The wind is blowing the leaves off the trees.*

blown See **blow**.
I've already blown the balloons up.

blunt adjective **blunter, bluntest**
Something like a knife or a pencil that is blunt is not sharp.

boat noun **boats**
A boat floats and carries people or things on water.

body noun **bodies**
The body of a person or animal is the whole of them.

boil verb **boils, boiling, boiled**
1 When water boils, it is very hot and you can see bubbles and steam.
2 When you boil something, you cook it in boiling water.

bone noun **bones**
Your bones are the hard white parts inside your body.

bonfire noun **bonfires**
A bonfire is a large fire that someone lights outdoors.

book noun **books**
A book has pages fixed inside a cover. Books have writing or pictures in them.

boot noun **boots**
1 A boot is a kind of shoe that comes up above your ankle.
2 A boot is also the place in a car where you put luggage.

a
b
c
d
e
f
g
h
i
j
k
l
m
n
o
p
q
r
s
t
u
v
w
x
y
z

bored adjective
If you are bored, you feel tired or irritated because you have nothing to do.

boring adjective
If something is boring, it is not interesting.

born
When a baby is born, it comes out of its mother's body. *My baby brother was born last week.*

borrow verb **borrows, borrowing, borrowed**
When you borrow something from somebody, you take it for a short time and promise to give it back later.

bottle noun **bottles**
A bottle is made to hold liquids. Bottles are made of glass or plastic.

bottom noun **bottoms**
1 The bottom is the lowest part of anything. *We rolled down to the bottom of the hill.*
2 Your bottom is the part of your body that you sit on.

bought See **buy**.
Dad bought me a new bike.

bounce verb **bounces, bouncing, bounced**
When something bounces, it comes back again after hitting something else. *The ball bounced off the ground and into the distance.*

bow ❶ noun **bows**
1 A bow is a knot you use to tie a ribbon.
2 A bow is also a bent piece of wood used for shooting arrows.

bow ❷ verb **bows, bowing, bowed**
If you bow, you bend over at the waist. *The red knight bowed to the king.*

bowl noun **bowls**
A bowl is a kind of deep plate that is made to hold things like soup, fruit, or breakfast cereals.

box noun **boxes**
A box has straight sides and is made to hold things. Most boxes are made from cardboard, wood, or plastic.

boy noun **boys**
A boy is a male child or young adult.

brain noun **brains**
Your brain is inside your head. You use your brain for thinking, remembering, and having feelings.

branch noun **branches**
A branch grows out from the trunk of a tree.

brave adjective **braver, bravest**
If you are brave, you show that you are not afraid.

a
b
c
d
e
f
g
h
i
j
k
l
m
n
o
p
q
r
s
t
u
v
w
x
y
z

bread noun
Bread is a food made by baking flour mixed with water.

break verb **breaks, breaking, broke, broken**
If something breaks, it goes into pieces or stops working. *Be careful, Dad, or you'll break a window with that ball.*

breakfast noun **breakfasts**
Breakfast is the first meal after you wake up in the morning.

breathe verb **breathes, breathing, breathed**
When you breathe, you take air in through your nose or mouth and then let it out again.

brick noun **bricks**
A brick is a small block of baked clay. Bricks are used for building.

bridge noun **bridges**
A bridge goes over a river, railway, or road, so that people or traffic can get across, or under, or through.

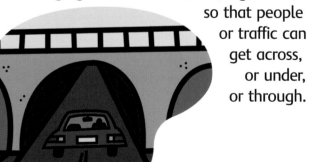

bright adjective **brighter, brightest**
1 Bright colours are strong and easy to see.
2 Bright lights shine strongly.
3 A person who is bright learns quickly.

bring verb **brings, bringing, brought**
If you bring something, you carry it here. *Don't forget to bring some food for our picnic.*

broke See **break**.
I dropped my glass and broke it.

broken See **break**.
Jamie has broken my watch.

broom noun **brooms**
A broom is a brush with a long handle. It is used for sweeping a floor or path.

brother noun **brothers**
Your brother is a boy who has the same parents as you do.

brought See **bring**.
I have brought you some flowers.

brush noun **brushes**
A brush has lots of short, stiff hairs, fixed into a handle made of wood or plastic.

bubble noun **bubbles**
A bubble is a small ball of soap or liquid with air inside.

bucket noun **buckets**
A bucket has a handle and is used to carry liquids or sand.

build verb **builds, building, built**
If you build something, you make it by putting different parts together. *I'm building a robot.*

building noun **buildings**
A building has walls and a roof. Houses, factories, and schools are buildings.

built See **build**.
A bird built a nest in the old tree.

bulb noun **bulbs**
1 A bulb is the glass part of a lamp that gives light.
2 A bulb can also be the root of a flower. Daffodils and tulips grow from bulbs.

bull noun **bulls**
A bull is a large male animal of the cow family.

bump noun **bumps**
A bump is a round lump on something. *Andy fell over and got a bump on his head.*

burn verb **burns, burning, burnt, burned**
1 If something is burning, it is on fire.
2 If someone burns something, they damage it with fire or heat. *Try not to burn the toast this time.*

burst verb **bursts, bursting, burst**
When something bursts, it breaks open suddenly. *The bag burst and all the apples fell on to the floor.*

bus noun **buses**
Buses are big vehicles that can carry lots of people to and from places.

bush noun **bushes**
A bush is like a small tree, with lots of branches.

busy adjective **busier, busiest**
1 Someone who is busy has a lot to do. *I can't help you just yet – I'm busy.*
2 When a place is busy, there's a lot going on. *The supermarket was busy today.*

butter noun
Butter is a yellow food that is made from cream. You can spread it on bread or cook with it.

butterfly noun **butterflies**
A butterfly is an insect with four large wings.

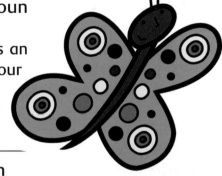

button noun **buttons**
Buttons are small, round objects sewn on to clothes. They fit into holes or loops to keep clothes done up.

buy verb **buys, buying, bought**
When you buy something, you pay money to have it.

buzz verb **buzzes, buzzing, buzzed**
If something buzzes, it makes a humming sound like a bee makes.

a b c d e f g h i j k l m n o p q r s t u v w x y z

15

call verb **calls, calling, called**
1 If you call someone, you speak loudly so that they will come to you. *Didn't you hear me call you?*
2 If a person or thing is called something, that is their name. *We have a dog called Razzle.*

came See **come**.
All my friends came for a sleepover.

camera noun **cameras**
You use a camera to take photos.

camp noun **camps**
A camp is a group of tents or huts where people live for a short time.

can ❶ verb
If you can do something, you are able to do it. *I can touch my nose with my tongue.*

can ❷ noun **cans**
A can is made of metal. You can buy food or drink in cans.

candle noun **candles**
A candle is a stick of wax with string through the middle. You can set the string on fire and it gives light.

can't verb
If you can't do something, you are not able to do it. *I can't read your writing.*

car noun **cars**
You can ride in a car. It has wheels and an engine to make it go.

cage noun **cages**
A cage is a box or room with bars. Pets like mice live in cages.

cake noun **cakes**
A cake is food made with flour, butter, eggs, and sugar. You bake a cake in the oven.

calculator noun **calculators**
A calculator is a machine that you use to solve maths problems.

calendar noun **calendars**
A calendar is a list showing all the days, weeks, and months in a year.

calf noun **calves**
1 A calf is a young cow or bull.
2 Your calf is at the back of your leg, between your knee and your ankle.

a b c d e f g h i j k l m n o p q r s t u v w x y z

card noun **cards**

1 Card is thick, stiff paper.
2 A greetings card has a picture and words on it. You send cards to people at special times, like birthdays.

3 Playing cards have numbers or pictures on them. You play games with them.

cardboard noun

Cardboard is very thick, strong paper.

care verb **cares, caring, cared**

1 If you care for something, you look after it. *My grandpa taught me how to care for pet fish.*
2 If you care about something, you think it matters. *She cares a lot about the environment.*

careful adjective

If you are careful, you think about what you are doing and try to do it safely and well. *Be careful when you cross the road.*

carpet noun **carpets**

A carpet is a thick cover for the floor.

carry verb **carries, carrying, carried**

If you carry something, you take it from one place to another. *The lion carried the cub in its mouth.*

carton noun **cartons**

A carton is made of thin cardboard or plastic. You can buy food or drink in cartons.

cartoon noun **cartoons**

1 A cartoon is a film that uses drawings instead of actors.
2 A cartoon is also a funny drawing.

case noun **cases**

You can keep or carry things in a case. There are cases to hold things like pencils or clothes.

castle noun **castles**

A castle is a large, strong building with very thick stone walls and tall towers. Castles were built long ago to keep the people inside safe from their enemies.

cat noun **cats**

A cat is a furry animal. Small cats are often kept as pets. Large cats like lions and tigers live in the wild.

catch verb **catches, catching, caught**

1 When you catch something that is moving, you get hold of it. *I'll throw the ball and you catch it.*
2 If you catch a bus, you are on time to get on it.
3 If you catch an illness, you become ill with it.

a b c d e f g h i j k l m n o p q r s t u v w x y z

caterpillar noun **caterpillars**
A caterpillar is a long, creeping creature that will turn into a butterfly or moth.

caught See **catch**.
Tommy caught the ball in one hand.

cave noun **caves**
A cave is a big hole under the ground or inside a mountain.

CD noun **CDs**
CD is short for compact disc. CDs hold music or information. You play them on a CD player or computer.

ceiling noun **ceilings**
A ceiling is the part of a room above your head.

cereal noun **cereals**
1 A cereal is a kind of grass grown by farmers for its seeds. *Rice and wheat are cereals.*
2 A cereal is also a kind of breakfast food that you eat with milk.

chain noun **chains**
A chain is a number of rings joined together in a line.

chair noun **chairs**
A chair is a seat with a back and sometimes arms, for one person.

chalk noun **chalks**
1 Chalk is a soft white rock. *The cliffs here are made of chalk.*
2 Chalks are pieces of soft white rock that you write or draw with on a blackboard.

change ❶ verb **changes, changing, changed**
When things change, they become different. *As tadpoles grow, they change into frogs.*

change ❷ noun
Change is the money you get back when you have paid more than something costs.

chapter noun **chapters**
A chapter is a part of a book.

charge noun
Someone who is in charge of something makes sure that it is looked after. *Mrs Dodds is in charge of the library at school.*

chase verb **chases, chasing, chased**
When you chase somebody, you run after them and try to catch them.

cheap adjective **cheaper, cheapest**
Something cheap does not cost very much. *I like the red shoes, but the blue ones are cheaper.*

cheek noun **cheeks**
Your cheeks are the soft parts on each side of your face.

cheer verb **cheers, cheering, cheered**
When people cheer, they shout to show they like something. *At the end of the show, everyone cheered and clapped.*

cheese noun
Cheese is a food. There are lots of different kinds of cheese, but they are all made from milk.

cheetah noun **cheetahs**
A cheetah is a big wild cat with spots on its coat. Cheetahs are the world's fastest animals on land.

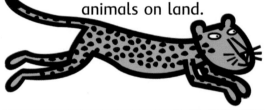

chew verb **chews, chewing, chewed**
When you chew food, you use your teeth to break it up into smaller pieces.

chick noun **chicks**
A chick is a baby bird.

chicken noun **chickens**
A chicken is a bird that farmers keep. Chickens lay eggs that we eat.

child noun **children**
A child is a young boy or girl.

chimney noun **chimneys**
A chimney is a long pipe that takes smoke from a fire up through the roof of a building.

chin noun **chins**
Your chin is the part of your face that is below your mouth.

chocolate noun **chocolates**
Chocolate is a sweet brown food or drink made from cocoa.

choose verb **chooses, choosing, chose, chosen**
If you choose something, you make up your mind which one you want. *I couldn't decide which cake to choose.*

chop verb **chops, chopping, chopped**
If you chop something, you cut it up with an axe or a knife. *He took an axe and chopped down the tree.*

chose See **choose**.
Luke chose a book on dinosaurs.

chosen See **choose**.
Have you chosen your pizza yet?

circle noun **circles**
A circle is a round shape like a ring.

circus noun **circuses**
A circus is a show in a big tent with clowns, acrobats, and sometimes animals that have been trained to do tricks.

a b c d e f g h i j k l m n o p q r s t u v w x y z

a
b
c
d
e
f
g
h
i
j
k
l
m
n
o
p
q
r
s
t
u
v
w
x
y
z

city noun **cities**
A city is a very big town.

clap verb **claps, clapping, clapped**
If you clap, you hit your hands together to make a noise. *Everyone started to clap at the end of the magic show.*

class noun **classes**
A class is a group of pupils who learn together.

claw noun **claws**
A claw is the sharp, curved nail on the foot of an animal or bird.

clean ❶ adjective **cleaner, cleanest**
Something that is clean has no dirty marks on it. *This floor is not very clean.*

clean ❷ verb **cleans, cleaning, cleaned**
When you clean something, you get all the dirt off it. *I clean my teeth twice a day.*

clear ❶ adjective **clearer, clearest**
1 If something is clear, it is easy to see, hear, or understand. *I found my way easily because the map was so clear.*
2 If something is clear, it is free of things you do not want. *If the road is clear, you can cross.*
3 If something like glass or plastic is clear, you can see through it. *The water is so clear, you can see the bottom of the pond.*

clear ❷ verb **clears, clearing, cleared**
When you clear a place, you take things away. *I'll help you clear the table.*

clever adjective **cleverer, cleverest**
Someone who is clever can learn and understand things easily.

cliff noun **cliffs**
A cliff is a hill with one side that goes straight down. Cliffs are often near the sea.

climb verb **climbs, climbing, climbed**
When you climb, you go up or down something high. *My sister and I like climbing the trees in our garden.*

cloak noun **cloaks**
A cloak is a very loose coat without sleeves.

clock noun **clocks**
A clock is a machine that shows you what the time is.

close adjective **closer, closest**
When something is close, it is near. *He lives in a red house close to the sea.*

close verb **closes, closing, closed**
When you close something, you shut it. *Close the window when you leave the room.*

cloth noun **cloths**
1 Cloth is material for making things like clothes and curtains.
2 A cloth is a piece of cloth for cleaning or covering something.

clothes noun
Clothes are the things that people wear.

cloud noun **clouds**
You can see clouds floating in the sky. They can be white or grey. Clouds are made of tiny drops of water that sometimes fall as rain.

clown noun **clowns**
A clown wears funny clothes, has a painted face, and does silly things to make people laugh.

coat noun **coats**
You put a coat on top of other clothes when you go outside. Coats have long sleeves.

cobweb noun **cobwebs**
A cobweb is a thin, sticky net made by a spider to catch insects.

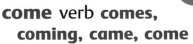

coin noun **coins**
A coin is a piece of metal money.

cold ❶ adjective **colder, coldest**
If you are cold, you feel that you want to put on warm clothes, or stand near something warm. *The weather got very cold and it began to snow.*

cold ❷ noun **colds**
A cold is an illness that makes you sneeze and your nose run.

collar ❶ noun **collars**
1 A collar is the part that goes round the neck of clothes like shirts and jackets.
2 A collar is also a band that goes round the neck of a dog or cat.

colour noun **colours**
Red, blue, and yellow are all colours. You can mix these together to get other colours.

come verb **comes, coming, came, come**
If you come to a place, you go towards it or arrive there. *Look, the ducks are coming towards us.*

comfortable adjective
If something is comfortable, it feels good to be in or to wear. *This chair is really comfortable.*

a
b
c
d
e
f
g
h
i
j
k
l
m
n
o
p
q
r
s
t
u
v
w
x
y
z

21

a b **c** d e f g h i j k l m n o p q r s t u v w x y z

comic noun **comics**
A comic is a paper with stories told in pictures.

computer noun **computers**
A computer is a machine that stores information. Computers can also work things out, or help other machines to work.

control verb **controls, controlling, controlled**
If you control something, you are in charge of it and make it do what you want. *Please try to control your dog.*

cook verb **cooks, cooking, cooked**
If someone cooks food, they get it ready to eat by heating it. *Let's cook pancakes today.*

cooker noun **cookers**
A cooker is a machine for cooking food. It has an oven below for baking, and places on top for boiling or frying.

cool adjective **cooler, coolest**
If something is cool, it feels fairly cold. *I'll put the orange juice in the fridge to keep it cool.*

copy verb **copies, copying, copied**
If you copy something, you do it exactly the same. *See if you can copy this picture of a horse.*

corner noun **corners**
A corner is the point where two sides, edges, or streets meet. *A square has four corners.*

cost verb **costs, costing, cost**
If something costs a particular amount, that is how much you have to pay to buy it. *How much does this football cost?*

cot noun **cots**
A cot is a bed for a baby. Cots have high sides to stop the baby falling out.

cotton noun
1 Cotton is a light material made from threads of the cotton plant.
2 Cotton is also a thread for sewing.

cough verb **coughs, coughing, coughed**
When you cough, you make a sudden loud noise with your throat. *Smoke from the bonfire made us cough.*

count verb **counts, counting, counted**
1 When you count, you say numbers in order. *You count up to fifty, and I'll hide.*
2 To count also means to use numbers to find out how many people or things there are. *The farmer is counting his sheep.*

country noun **countries**
1 A country is a land with its own people and laws. *France, the United States of America, and China are all countries.*
2 The country is land with farms and villages away from towns.

cousin noun **cousins**
Your cousin is the son or daughter of your aunt or uncle.

cover ❶ verb **covers, covering, covered**
If you cover something, you put another thing over or round it. *Before you start painting, cover the table with newspaper.*

cover ❷ noun **covers**
A cover is something that goes over or around something else.
My book has an elephant on the cover.

cow noun **cows**
A cow is a large female animal that gives milk.

crack noun **cracks**
1 A crack is a thin line on something where it has broken but not come to pieces.
2 A crack is also a sharp noise like the noise a dry twig makes when it breaks.

cracker noun **crackers**
1 A cracker is a thin biscuit.
2 A cracker is also a paper tube which bangs when two people pull it. *Our Christmas crackers had paper hats and jokes inside.*

crane noun **cranes**
1 A crane is a tall machine that lifts very heavy things.
2 A crane is also a large bird with very long legs. Cranes live near water.

crash ❶ verb **crashes, crashing, crashed**
When something crashes, it falls or hits something else with a loud noise. *Huge waves crashed against the side of the ship.*

crash ❷ noun **crashes**
1 A crash is a very loud noise. *The lightning was followed by a crash of thunder.*
2 A crash is also a traffic accident.

crawl verb **crawls, crawling, crawled**
When you crawl, you move along on your hands and knees.

crayon noun **crayons**
A crayon is a coloured pencil often made of wax.

cream noun
Cream is the thick, fatty part of milk, often used in cakes and puddings.

creature noun **creatures**
A creature is any animal. *This forest is full of strange creatures.*

creep verb **creeps, creeping, crept**
1 If you creep somewhere, you walk very slowly and quietly so no one will hear you. *I saw you creeping down the stairs.*
2 An animal that creeps moves along close to the ground.

crept See **creep**.
We were late and crept in at the back.

crew noun **crews**
A crew is the group of people who work on a ship or aeroplane.

cricket noun **crickets**
1 Cricket is a game played with a bat and ball. There are eleven players on each side.
2 A cricket is a jumping insect that makes a shrill sound.

crocodile noun **crocodiles**
A crocodile is a large reptile that lives in rivers in some hot countries.

crop noun **crops**
Crops are the plants that a farmer grows and sells for food.

cross ❶ adjective **crosser, crossest**
If you are cross, you feel annoyed about something.

cross ❷ noun **crosses**
A cross is a mark like this + or this x.

cross ❸ verb **crosses, crossing, crossed**
If you cross something like a river or road, you go from one side to the other. *Be careful when you cross the road.*

crowd noun **crowds**
A crowd is lots of people in one place.

crown noun **crowns**
A crown is a ring of gold and jewels that kings and queens wear on their heads.

crust noun **crusts**
A crust is the hard part on the outside of bread.

cry ❶ verb **cries, crying, cried**
When you cry, tears fall from your eyes. People cry when they are sad or hurt.

cry ❷ noun **cries**
A cry is a shout.

cub noun **cubs**
A cub is a young wild animal, especially a young lion, tiger, bear, or fox.

cuddle verb **cuddles, cuddling, cuddled**

If you cuddle someone, you hold them closely in your arms.

cup noun **cups**

People drink things like tea from a cup. A cup has a handle.

cupboard noun **cupboards**

A cupboard is a piece of furniture with a door at the front. You keep things in a cupboard.

curl ❶ noun **curls**

Curls are pieces of hair that grow or are twisted into rings.

curl ❷ verb **curls, curling, curled**

If you curl up, you sit or lie with your body bent round itself. *I curled up in the armchair in front of the fire.*

curtain noun **curtains**

A curtain is a piece of cloth that you pull across a window to cover it.

curved adjective

Something that is curved is not straight. *A parrot has a curved beak.*

cut ❶ verb **cuts, cutting, cut**

If you cut something, you use scissors or a knife. *I cut a sun out of yellow card.*

cut ❷ noun **cuts**

A cut is an opening in your skin made by something sharp.

a
b
c
d
e
f
g
h
i
j
k
l
m
n
o
p
q
r
s
t
u
v
w
x
y
z

25

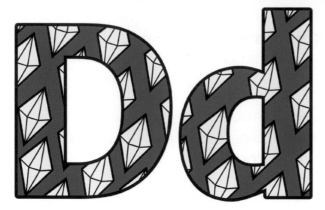

dad noun **dads**
Dad or daddy is what you call your father.

damage verb **damages, damaging, damaged**
If a person or thing damages something, they spoil it in some way. *The storm damaged lots of trees.*

damp adjective **damper, dampest**
Something that is damp is a little bit wet.

dance verb **dances, dancing, danced**
When you dance, you move about in time to music.

danger noun **dangers**
If there is danger, something bad might happen. *The sign by the pond said 'Danger – thin ice!'*

dangerous adjective
Something that is dangerous is likely to hurt you. *Crossing a busy road is dangerous.*

dark adjective **darker, darkest**
1 If it is dark, there is no light or not much light.
2 Dark hair is brown or black.

date noun **dates**
A date is the day, month, and sometimes the year when something happens.
Today's date is 20th June.

daughter noun **daughters**
A person's daughter is their female child.

day noun **days**
1 The day is the time when it is light, from when the sun comes up to when the sun goes down. *I've been working hard all day.*
2 A day is one of the twenty-four hours between one midnight and the next.

dead adjective
If someone or something is dead, they are no longer living.

a b c d e f g h i j k l m n o p q r s t u v w x y z

26

deaf adjective **deafer, deafest**
Someone who is deaf cannot hear well. Some deaf people cannot hear at all.

decide verb **decides, deciding, decided**
When you decide, you make up your mind about something. *I can't decide what to wear.*

decorate verb **decorates, decorating, decorated**
1 When you decorate something, you make it look pretty. *We decorated the tree.*
2 When people decorate a room, they make it look fresh by painting it or putting paper on the walls.

deep adjective **deeper, deepest**
Something that is deep goes a long way down from the top. *There was a deep well at the end of the garden.*

deer noun **deer**
A deer is a large animal that can run very fast. Male deer have big horns like branches on their heads, called antlers.

defend verb **defends, defending, defended**
To defend means to keep someone or something safe from attack. *We defended the castle from our enemies.*

delicious adjective
If something is delicious, it tastes or smells very nice.

deliver verb **delivers, delivering, delivered**
If someone delivers something, they bring it to you. *The postman delivered a parcel this morning.*

dentist noun **dentists**
A dentist's job is to take care of people's teeth.

describe verb **describes, describing, described**
If you describe something, you say what it is like.

desert noun **deserts**
A desert is a hot, dry land where few plants can grow.

desk noun **desks**
A desk is a kind of table where you can read, write, draw, or use a computer.

destroy verb **destroys, destroying, destroyed**
If you destroy something, you damage it so much that it can no longer be used.

diamond noun **diamonds**
A diamond is a hard, sparkling jewel that is clear like glass.

a b c **d** e f g h i j k l m n o p q r s t u v w x y z

a
b
c
d
e
f
g
h
i
j
k
l
m
n
o
p
q
r
s
t
u
v
w
x
y
z

diary noun **diaries**
A diary is a book in which you can write down what happens each day.

dice noun **dice**
Dice are small cubes with dots on each face. You throw dice in some games.

dictionary noun **dictionaries**
A dictionary is a book where you can find out what a word means and how to spell it. The words in a dictionary are usually listed in alphabetical order.

did See **do**.
I did a project on rainforests last year.

die verb **dies, dying, died**
When a person, animal, or plant dies, they stop living. *Plants die when they don't have enough water.*

different adjective
If something is different from something else, it is not the same. *All the pencils in the box are different colours.*

difficult adjective
Something that is difficult is not easy to do or understand.

dig verb **digs, digging, dug**
To dig means to move soil away to make a hole in the ground.
The dog dug a hole to bury his bone.

dinner noun **dinners**
Dinner is the main meal of the day.

dinosaur noun **dinosaurs**
A dinosaur is a large reptile that lived millions of years ago.

direction noun **directions**
1 A direction is the way you go to get somewhere. *The beach is in that direction.*
2 Directions are words or pictures that tell you what to do or how to get somewhere. *Can you give me directions to the zoo?*

dirt noun
Dirt is dust, mud, or earth.

dirty adjective **dirtier, dirtiest**
Something that is dirty is covered with mud, food, or other marks.

disappear verb **disappears, disappearing, disappeared**
If something disappears, you cannot see it any longer. *After two days, my spots disappeared.*

disappointed adjective
If you are disappointed, you feel sad because something you were hoping for did not happen.

28

disaster noun **disasters**
A disaster is something very bad that happens suddenly.

discover verb **discovers, discovering, discovered**
When you discover something, you find out about it or see it for the first time. *I've discovered a secret drawer.*

discuss verb **discusses, discussing, discussed**
When people discuss things, they talk about them.

disguise noun **disguises**
A disguise is something you wear so that people will not know who you are.

dish noun **dishes**
A dish is for cooking or serving food.

disk noun **disks**
A disk is a thin, flat object that you use in a computer to store information.

distance noun **distances**
The distance between two places or things is how far they are from each other. *The distance from my house to my school is half a mile.*

dive verb **dives, diving, dived**
If you dive, you jump head first into water. *Serena dived off the top diving board.*

divide verb **divides, dividing, divided**
1 If you divide something, you make it into smaller pieces. *Divide the cake into six pieces.*
2 When you divide numbers, you find out how many times one goes into another. *Six divided by two is three.*

$$6 \div 2 = 3$$

do verb **does, doing, did, done**
When you do something, you finish it or spend time on it. *Alex likes to do jigsaws.*

doctor noun **doctors**
A doctor is someone whose job is to help people who are sick or hurt to get better.

does See **do**.
I like to watch while Grandma does the baking.

dog noun **dogs**
A dog is an animal that people keep as a pet or to do work.

doing See **do**.
What are you doing?

doll noun **dolls**
A doll is a toy that looks like a baby or a small person.

a
b
c
d
e
f
g
h
i
j
k
l
m
n
o
p
q
r
s
t
u
v
w
x
y
z

a
b
c
d
e
f
g
h
i
j
k
l
m
n
o
p
q
r
s
t
u
v
w
x
y
z

dolphin noun **dolphins**
A dolphin is an animal that lives in the sea. Dolphins are very clever and friendly.

done See **do**.
Have you done your teeth yet?

donkey noun **donkeys**
A donkey is an animal that looks like a small horse with long ears.

don't
Don't is short for do not. *I don't like spiders.*

door noun **doors**
A door closes or opens the entrance to something like a house or a room.

drag verb **drags, dragging, dragged**
If you drag something, you pull it along the ground.

dragon noun **dragons**
In stories, a dragon is a monster that has wings and can breathe out fire.

drain noun **drains**
A drain is a pipe that carries away water.

drank See **drink**.
I was so thirsty I drank two whole glasses of lemonade.

draw ❶ verb **draws, drawing, drew, drawn**
When you draw, you make a picture with a pen, pencil, or crayon.

draw ❷ noun **draws**
If a game ends in a draw, both sides have the same score.

drawer noun **drawers**
A drawer is a box for keeping things in that slides in and out of a piece of furniture.

drawing noun **drawings**
A drawing is a picture made with a pen, pencil, or crayon.

drawn See **draw**.
I've drawn a funny monster.

dream verb **dreams, dreaming, dreamed, dreamt**
When you dream, you see and hear things in your mind while you are asleep. *Last night I dreamed I could fly.*

30

dress ❶ noun **dresses**
A dress is something that girls and women wear. It is like a skirt and top in one.

dress ❷ verb **dresses, dressing, dressed**
When you dress, you put your clothes on. *I'll help you dress the baby.*

drew See **draw**.
Ben drew a picture of a clown.

drink ❶ verb **drinks, drinking, drank, drunk**
When you drink, you swallow liquid. *Would you like something to drink?*

drink ❷ noun **drinks**
A drink is a liquid that you swallow.

drip verb **drips, dripping, dripped**
When liquid drips, it falls in drops. *I left the tap dripping after my bath.*

drive verb **drives, driving, drove, driven**
When someone drives a car, a tractor, or a bus, they make it go where they want.

driven See **drive**.
My sister has never driven on her own before.

drop ❶ noun **drops**
A drop is a tiny amount of liquid.

drop verb **drops, dropping, dropped**
If you drop something, you let it fall. *I dropped all the eggs on the floor.*

drown verb **drowns, drowning, drowned**
If someone drowns, they die under water because they cannot breathe.

drum noun **drums**
A drum is a musical instrument that you play by hitting it with a stick.

drunk See **drink**.
I've already drunk my orange juice.

dry adjective **drier, driest**
Something that is dry is not damp or wet. *Your socks are dry enough to put on.*

duck noun **ducks**
A duck is a bird that lives near water. It has webbed feet for swimming.

dust noun
Dust is dry dirt like a powder.

a b c d e f g h i j k l m n o p q r s t u v w x y z

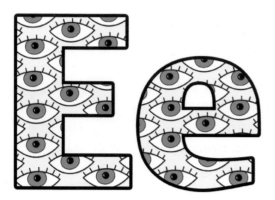

a b c d e f g h i j k l m n o p q r s t u v w x y z

eagle noun eagles
An eagle is a large bird with a curved beak. Eagles have their nests in high places like mountains.

ear noun ears
Your ears are the two parts of your body that you use for hearing.

early adjective earlier, earliest
1 Early means near the beginning of something. *The farmer milks the cows in the early morning.*
2 If someone is early, they arrive before you expect them. *You're too early – come back later.*

earn verb earns, earning, earned
If you earn money, you work for it.

earth noun
1 The Earth is the planet that we live on.

2 Earth is the soil or dirt that plants grow in. *In the spring, the seeds in the earth begin to grow.*

east noun
East is the direction of the rising sun. **E** is east.

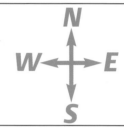

easy adjective easier, easiest
If something is easy, you can do it or understand it without any trouble.

eat verb eats, eating, ate, eaten
When you eat, you take food into your body. *Squirrels like to eat nuts.*

echo noun echoes
An echo is a sound that you hear again when it bounces back off something solid. *Jake shouted 'Hello!' in the cave and heard the echo 'Hello!' come back to him.*

edge noun edges
An edge is the part along the end or side of something.

effect noun effects
An effect is anything that happens because of something else. *The effect of all the rain was a flood.*

effort noun efforts
Effort is the hard work you put into something you are trying to do. *Beth made a real effort to write neatly.*

egg noun eggs
Baby birds, reptiles, amphibians, fish, and insects live inside eggs until they are big enough to be born. Birds' eggs are oval, with a thin, hard shell.

eight noun eights
Eight is the number 8.

elastic noun
Elastic is a strip of material than can be pulled to make it longer. When you let it go, it goes back to its usual size.

elbow noun elbows
Your elbow is the bony part in the middle of your arm, where it bends.

electricity noun
Electricity is power that moves along wires. It is used to give light and heat, and to make machines work.

elephant noun elephants
An elephant is a very large, grey animal with a very long nose, called a trunk and big ears.

eleven noun elevens
Eleven is the number 11.

empty adjective emptier, emptiest
Something that is empty has nothing in it.
The treasure chest was empty.

end ❶ noun ends
The end is the last part of something.
I read the book right to the end.

end ❷ verb ends, ending, ended
If something ends, it finishes or stops.
What time does the film end?

enemy noun enemies
An enemy is a person who wants to hurt or fight you.

energy noun
1 If you have energy, you can move quickly and do a lot of things. *Samir has lots of energy, he's always running around.*
2 Energy is the power to make machines work.

a
b
c
d
e
f
g
h
i
j
k
l
m
n
o
p
q
r
s
t
u
v
w
x
y
z

a b c d **e** f g h i j k l m n o p q r s t u v w x y z

engine noun **engines**
An engine is a machine that uses fuel to make things move. *The driver started the engine and the bus moved off.*

enjoy verb **enjoys, enjoying, enjoyed**
If you enjoy something, you like doing it. *I enjoy playing football with my friends.*

enormous adjective
Something enormous is very big.

enough
If you have enough of something, you do not need any more. *Have you had enough to eat?*

enter verb **enters, entering, entered**
If you enter a place, you go into it.

entrance noun **entrances**
The entrance to a place is the way in.

envelope noun **envelopes**
An envelope is a paper cover for a letter.

environment noun **environments**
The environment is the air, land, and water that surrounds us. *We are learning about protecting the environment.*

equal verb **equals, equalling, equalled**
If something equals something else, the two things are the same size or the same number. *Two plus two equals four.*

$$2+2=4$$

equipment noun
Equipment is all the things you need for doing something. *Our school has lots of sports equipment.*

escape verb **escapes, escaping, escaped**
If a person or animal escapes, they get away from something. *My rabbit keeps escaping from its cage.*

even adjective
1 If a number is even, it can be divided by two, with nothing left over. *Two, four, and six are even numbers.*
2 If two scores are even, they are the same.
3 If a path is even, it is flat and smooth.

evening noun **evenings**
The evening is the time at the end of the day when the sun sets, before people go to bed.

excellent adjective
Excellent means very good.

excited adjective
If you are excited, you are very happy about something and really looking forward to it.

excuse noun **excuses**
An excuse is what you say to explain why you have done something so that you will not get into trouble.

exercise noun **exercises**
1 Exercise is moving your body to keep fit. *Swimming is good exercise.*
2 An exercise is a piece of work you do to help you learn.

exit noun **exits**
An exit is the way out of a place.

expect verb **expects, expecting, expected**
If you expect something, you think it is very likely to happen. *I expect we will lose again.*

expensive adjective
Something expensive costs a lot of money.

explain verb **explains, explaining, explained**
If you explain something, you make it clear so that people can understand it. *Can you explain what makes a rainbow appear in the sky?*

explode verb **explodes, exploding, exploded**
When something explodes, it blows up with a very loud bang.

explore verb **explores, exploring, explored**
When you explore, you look carefully round a place for the first time.

extinct adjective
If a kind of animal is extinct, there are none living any more. *Dinosaurs have been extinct for millions of years.*

extra adjective
Extra means more than usual. *You should take extra sweaters in case the weather turns cold.*

eye noun **eyes**
Your eyes are the two parts of your body that you use for seeing.

a
b
c
d
e
f
g
h
i
j
k
l
m
n
o
p
q
r
s
t
u
v
w
x
y
z

a
b
c
d
e
f
g
h
i
j
k
l
m
n
o
p
q
r
s
t
u
v
w
x
y
z

face noun **faces**
Your face is the front
part of your head.

factory noun **factories**
A factory is a building where people and
machines make a large number of things.

fail verb **fails, failing, failed**
If someone fails, they try to do
something but cannot do it. *The pirates
failed to find the treasure and had to leave
without it.*

fair ❶ adjective **fairer, fairest**
1 Something that is fair seems right
because everyone is treated the same
way. *It's not fair! Why does she always
sit in the front?*
2 Fair can mean light in colour. *My sister
has long, fair hair.*

fair ❷ noun **fairs**
Fairs are set up with things like stalls,
roundabouts, and other rides so that
people can have fun.

fairy noun **fairies**
In stories, fairies are tiny people who
have wings and can do magic.

fall verb **falls, falling,
fell, fallen**
When something falls,
it comes down suddenly.
The apple fell from the branch.

fallen See **fall**.
I've fallen over and hurt my knee.

family noun **families**
A family is made up of parents, children,
and grandchildren.

famous adjective
Famous people and things
are very well known.

far adjective **farther,
farthest**
Something that is
far away is a long
way away.

farm noun **farms**
A farm is a piece of land for growing
crops or keeping animals for food.

fast adjective **faster, fastest**
Something that is fast can move quickly.

fasten verb **fastens, fastening,
fastened**
If you fasten something, you do it up.
You need to fasten your seatbelt.

36

fat ❶ adjective **fatter, fattest**
A person or animal that is fat has a very thick, round body.

fat ❷ noun **fats**
Fat is something like butter or oil that can be used in cooking.

father noun **fathers**
A father is a man who has a son or a daughter.

fault noun **faults**
If something bad is your fault, you made it happen.

favourite adjective
Your favourite is the one you like best. *My favourite meal is pizza.*

fear noun **fears**
Fear is the feeling you get when you think something bad is going to happen to you.

feast noun **feasts**
A feast is a special meal for a lot of people.

feather noun **feathers**
A feather is one of the soft, light things that cover a bird and help it to fly.

fed See **feed**.
We fed the ducks on the pond.

feed verb **feeds, feeding, fed**
If you feed a person or animal, you give them food. *Will you feed the dog, please?*

feel verb **feels, feeling, felt**
1 If you feel something, you touch it to find out what it is like. *Just feel how soft this kitten is!*
2 If you feel a particular way, like excited or tired, that is how you are at the time. *I feel sad now that I'm leaving.*

fell See **fall**.
The apple almost hit me when it fell.

felt See **feel**.
After swimming all afternoon I felt very tired.

female noun **females**
A female is a person or animal that belongs to the sex that can have babies. Girls and women are female.

fence noun **fences**
A fence is a kind of wall made of wood or wire. People put fences around gardens and fields.

fetch verb **fetches, fetching, fetched**
When you fetch something, you go and get it.

few adjective **fewer, fewest**
Few means not many. *I only have a few sweets left.*

field noun **fields**
A field is a piece of land with a fence or hedge around it. Farmers grow crops or grass in fields.

fierce adjective **fiercer, fiercest**
A fierce animal looks angry and might attack you.

fight verb **fights, fighting, fought**
When people or animals fight, they try to hurt each other.

fill verb **fills, filling, filled**
If you fill something, you put so much into it that you cannot get any more in. *Rose filled her cup to the top.*

film noun **films**
A film is also a story told in moving pictures. You watch a film at the cinema or on television.

fin noun **fins**
A fin is one of the thin, flat parts that stand out from a fish's body. Fins help fish to swim.

find verb **finds, finding, found**
When you find something that has been lost, you get it back. *I can't find my other sock.*

fine ❶ adjective **finer, finest**
1 Fine threads are very thin.
2 Fine weather is dry and sunny.
3 If you say you are fine, you mean you are well and happy.

fine ❷ noun **fines**
A fine is money that someone has to pay as a punishment.

finger noun **fingers**
Your fingers are the five long, thin parts at the end of your hand.

finish verb **finishes, finishing, finished**
When you finish, you come to the end of something. *Tara finished first and won the race.*

fire noun **fires**
1 Fire is the heat, flames, and bright light that comes from something that is burning. *Wild animals are afraid of fire.*
2 A fire is something that keeps people warm. *Grandpa was sitting by the fire.*

fire engine noun **fire engines**
A fire engine is a large truck that takes fire fighters, hoses and ladders to a fire.

firework noun **fireworks**
A firework is a paper tube filled with powder. When you light it, the firework makes a loud bang or burns with coloured sparks or flames.

firm adjective **firmer, firmest**
If something is firm, it is hard or is fixed so that it will not give way.

first

If something or someone is first, they come before all the others.

fish ❶ noun fish fishes

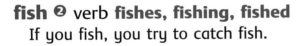

A fish is an animal that lives and breathes under water.
Fish are covered with scales, and they have fins and a tail for swimming.

fish ❷ verb fishes, fishing, fished

If you fish, you try to catch fish.

fit ❶ verb fits, fitting, fitted

If something fits you, it is the right size and shape. *The coat fitted me perfectly.*

fit ❷ adjective fitter, fittest

Someone who is fit is healthy.

five noun fives

Five is the number 5.

fix verb fixes, fixing, fixed

1 If you fix something that is broken, you mend it.
2 If you fix something somewhere, you join it firmly to something else.

fizzy adjective fizzier, fizziest

A fizzy drink is one that is full of little bubbles.

flag noun flags

A flag is a piece of cloth with a pattern on it. It is used as a symbol of a country or a group of people.

flame noun flames

A flame is one of the hot, bright strips of light you see rising up from a fire.

flap verb flaps, flapping, flapped

When a bird flaps its wings, it moves them up and down quickly.

flash noun flashes

A flash is a sudden bright light. *A flash of lightning lit up the sky.*

flat ❶ adjective flatter, flattest

Something that is flat does not slope or have any bumps or wrinkles. The top of a table is flat.

flat ❷ noun flats

A flat is a home. It is a set of rooms inside a house or big building.

flavour noun flavours

The flavour of food or drink is what it tastes like.

flew See fly.

A helicopter flew over our heads.

flipper noun flippers

The flippers on animals such as seals, turtles, or penguins are the flat arms that they use for swimming.

a
b
c
d
e
f
g
h
i
j
k
l
m
n
o
p
q
r
s
t
u
v
w
x
y
z

float verb **floats, floating, floated**
1 If something floats, it stays on top of a liquid.
2 If something floats through the air, it drifts along gently.

flock noun **flocks**
A flock is a group of birds or sheep.

floor noun **floors**
A floor is the part of a room or building that people walk on.

flour noun
Flour is a powder made from wheat that you use to make bread and cakes.

flow verb **flows, flowing, flowed**
To flow means to move along like water. *The stream flows very fast here.*

flower noun **flowers**
A flower is the part of a plant that makes seeds. Many flowers are brightly coloured.

flown See **fly.**
The birds have flown away.

fly ❶ verb **flies, flying, flew, flown**
1 When something flies, it moves through the air.
2 When people fly, they travel in an aircraft. *We are flying to Dublin tomorrow.*

fly ❷ noun **flies**
A fly is a small insect with one pair of wings.

fog noun
Fog is a thick cloud that is close to the ground and difficult to see through.

fold verb **folds, folding, folded**
If you fold something, you bend it so that one part goes over another. *Josh folded the letter and put it in an envelope.*

follow verb **follows, following, followed**
If you follow someone, you go after them. *The little lamb followed her everywhere she went.*

food noun
Food is anything that you eat to help you grow and be healthy.

foot noun **feet**
Your feet are the parts of your body at the end of your legs that you stand on.

football noun **footballs**
1 Football is a game played by two teams who kick a ball and try to score goals.
2 A football is a large ball that you use to play football.

forest noun **forests**
A forest is a place where a lot of trees are growing together.

forever adverb
Forever means always.

forgave See **forgive**.
My sister broke my doll, but I forgave her because it was an accident.

forget verb **forgets, forgetting, forgot, forgotten**
If you forget something, you do not remember it. *I'm always forgetting my football boots.*

forgive verb **forgives, forgiving, forgave, forgiven**
If you forgive someone, you stop being angry with them. *Please forgive me for missing your birthday party.*

forgiven See **forgive**.
I have forgiven you for losing my pen.

forgot See **forget**.
I forgot to take my lunch to school, so I was hungry all afternoon.

forgotten See **forget**.
I know that boy but I've forgotten his name.

fork noun **forks**
A fork is a tool with three or four thin pointed parts. People use small forks for eating and large forks for digging in the garden.

fortnight noun **fortnights**
A fortnight is two weeks.

fought See **fight**.
The two armies fought each other all day.

found See **find**.
I've found my other shoe at last!

four noun **fours**
Four is the number 4.

fox noun **foxes**
A fox is a wild animal that looks like a dog with a long furry tail.

frame noun **frames**
A frame is something that fits round the edge of a picture or window.

free adjective **freer, freest**
1 If you are free, you can do what you like or go where you like.
2 Free things do not cost anything. *Children under five can get in free.*

freeze verb **freezes, freezing, froze, frozen**
1 When water freezes, it changes into ice.
2 People freeze food to keep it from going bad.
3 If you say you are freezing, you mean you are very cold.

fresh adjective **fresher, freshest**
1 Fresh food has just been picked or made.
2 Fresh water is not salty.
3 Fresh air is clean and pure.

a
b
c
d
e
f
g
h
i
j
k
l
m
n
o
p
q
r
s
t
u
v
w
x
y
z

fridge noun **fridges**
A fridge is a metal cupboard that uses electricity to keep food cold and fresh.

friend noun **friends**
A friend is someone you know well and like and who likes you too.

friendly adjective **friendlier, friendliest**
Someone who is friendly is kind and helpful.

frighten verb **frightens, frightening, frightened**
If something frightens a person or animal, it makes them feel afraid.

frog noun **frogs**
A frog is a small animal with a smooth, wet skin. Frogs live near water and have strong back legs for jumping.

front noun **fronts**
The front of anything is the side that people usually see first. *She spilled some juice down the front of her dress.*

frown verb **frowns, frowning, frowned**
When you frown, you look cross or worried and lines come onto your forehead.

froze See **freeze**.
It was so cold that the pond froze.

frozen See **freeze**.
A couple of ducks were standing on the frozen pond.

fruit noun **fruits**
Fruit is something like an apple, orange, or banana which grows on a bush or tree. Fruits have seeds in them.

fry verb **fries, frying, fried**
When you fry food, you cook it in hot oil or fat in a pan.

full adjective **fuller, fullest**
If something is full, there is no more room in it. *The chest was full of gold coins.*

fun noun
When you have fun, you enjoy yourself and feel happy.

funny adjective **funnier, funniest**
1 If something is funny, it makes you laugh. *Do you know any funny jokes?*
2 Something funny seems strange. *What's that funny smell?*

fur noun
Fur is the thick soft hair that covers some animals.

furniture noun
Furniture is all the big things like beds, tables, chairs, and cupboards that you need in a house.

furry adjective
A furry animal is covered in thick, soft hair.

future noun
The future is the time that will come. *In the future, we could all be driving space ships instead of cars.*

gale noun **gales**
A gale is a
very strong wind.

game noun **games**
A game is something you play that
has rules. Football,
chess, snakes and
ladders, and
hide-and-seek
are games.

gap noun **gaps**
A gap is a space between two things.
The dog squeezed through a gap in the fence.

garage noun **garages**
1 A garage is a building where
you keep a car.
2 A garage is also a place
that sells fuel or repairs cars.

garden noun **gardens**
A garden is a piece of ground where
people can grow flowers and
vegetables. Someone's garden
is usually next to their house.

gas noun **gases**
A gas is anything like air, that is not
solid or liquid. Some gases have strong
smells. Some gases burn easily and are
used for heating and cooking.

gate noun **gates**
A gate is a kind of door in a wall, fence,
or hedge.

gave See **give**.
Grandpa gave me a football for my birthday.

gentle adjective **gentler, gentlest**
If you are gentle, you are kind, quiet,
and careful.

get verb **gets, getting, got**
If you get something, you go to where
it is and bring it back.

ghost noun **ghosts**
A ghost is the spirit of a
dead person that some people
believe they have seen.

giant noun **giants**
A giant is a huge person
in fairy tales.

giraffe noun **giraffes**
A giraffe is a very tall animal with a
long neck and long, thin legs.

girl noun **girls**
A girl is a female child or young adult.

a
b
c
d
e
f
g
h
i
j
k
l
m
n
o
p
q
r
s
t
u
v
w
x
y
z

a
b
c
d
e
f
g
h
i
j
k
l
m
n
o
p
q
r
s
t
u
v
w
x
y
z

give verb **gives, giving, gave, given**
If you give something to someone, you let them have it. *We are going to give Mum a ride in a hot air balloon for her birthday.*

given See **give**.
I've already given you two biscuits.

glad adjective **gladder, gladdest**
If you are glad, you are happy about something.

glass noun **glasses**
1 Glass is hard material that you can see through. It is used to make windows and bottles.
2 A glass is a kind of cup made of glass.

glasses noun
People wear glasses in front of their eyes to help them see better. Glasses are two pieces of glass or plastic in a frame.

glove noun **gloves**
A glove is a covering for the hand with places for the thumb and each finger.

glue noun
Glue is a thick liquid used for sticking things together.

go verb **goes, going, went, gone**
If you go somewhere, you move from one place to another. *Let's all go to the park.*

goal noun **goals**
1 A goal is the two posts that a ball must go between to score a point in games like football.
2 A goal is also a point that is scored when a ball goes into the goal.

goat noun **goats**
A goat is an animal with horns and sometimes a beard under its chin. Goats are sometimes kept for their milk.

going
If you are going to do something, you are about to do it.

gold noun
Gold is a valuable yellow metal that can be made into jewellery.

goldfish noun **goldfish**
A goldfish is a small orange fish often kept as a pet.

gone See **go**.
Everyone has gone home.

good adjective **better, best**
1 If you say something is good, you like it.
2 Work that is good is done well.
3 If you are good, you behave well.
4 A good person is kind and caring.

44

goodbye
You say goodbye when you leave someone.

goose noun **geese**
A goose is a large bird with a long neck that lives near water.

gorilla noun **gorillas**
A gorilla is a large, strong ape.

got See **get**.
Amy got her coat from the car.

grain noun **grains**
A grain of rice, wheat, or other cereal is a seed from the plant.

grandfather noun **grandfathers**
Your grandfather is the father of your father or mother. You can also call him your grandpa.

grandmother noun **grandmothers**
Your grandmother is the mother of your father or mother. You can also call her your grandma.

grass noun
Grass is a green plant with thin leaves. There are usually lots of these plants growing close together in gardens and fields.

great adjective
1 Great means very good. *We all had a great time at the party.*
2 Great also means large. *The prince lived in a great big house.*

greedy adjective **greedier, greediest**
Someone who is greedy wants more than their fair share of money or food.

grew See **grow**.
The beanstalk grew right up into the sky.

ground noun
The ground is the earth or other surface that you walk on outside.

group noun **groups**
A group is a number of people or things that are all together or belong together.

grow verb **grows, growing, grew, grown**
When somebody or something grows, they get bigger.

guess verb **guesses, guessing, guessed**
When you guess, you give the answer to something without really knowing if it is right.
Can you guess what's in the box?

guitar noun **guitars**
A guitar is a musical instrument with strings. You play it with your fingers.

a
b
c
d
e
f
g
h
i
j
k
l
m
n
o
p
q
r
s
t
u
v
w
x
y
z

45

a
b
c
d
e
f
g
h
i
j
k
l
m
n
o
p
q
r
s
t
u
v
w
x
y
z

had See **have**.
Amy had a bad cold last week.

hair noun
Hair is the soft covering that grows on your head and body.

half noun **halves**
A half is one of two equal parts.
Let's cut the pizza in half.

hamster noun **hamsters**
A hamster is a small furry animal, with places inside its cheeks where it can hold food. Hamsters are often kept as pets.

hand noun **hands**
Your hands are the parts of your body that you use for holding things. A hand has four fingers and a thumb.

handle noun **handles**
A handle is the part of something that you use to hold or carry it. Cups, baskets, saucepans, and doors have handles.

hang verb **hangs, hanging, hung**
When you hang something, you fix the top of it to a hook or nail. *Please hang your coat up.*

happy adjective **happier, happiest**
When you are happy, you feel pleased about something.

hard adjective **harder, hardest**
1 Something that is hard is not soft.
2 Something that is hard to do is not easy.
This sum is too hard!

has See **have**.
Katie has three teddies.

hat noun **hats**
A hat is something you wear on your head.

hatch verb **hatches, hatching, hatched**
When a baby bird hatches, it breaks out of its egg.

hate verb **hates, hating, hated**
If you hate someone or something, you feel very strongly that you do not like them or it. *I hate getting up when it is still dark.*

46

have verb **has, having, had**
If you have something, it is with you or you own or feel it. *I have a new bike. I have a headache.*

having See **have**.
We are having a picnic tomorrow.

hay noun
Hay is dry grass that is used to feed animals.

head noun **heads**
1 Your head is the part of your body that is above your neck and has your brain in it.
2 The head of something like a school is the person in charge.

healthy adjective **healthier, healthiest**
1 If you feel healthy, you feel well and full of energy.
2 Healthy things are good for you.

hear verb **hears, hearing, heard**
When you hear, you take in sounds through your ears. *Can you hear that dog barking?*

heart noun **hearts**
Your heart is a part of your body inside your chest. It pumps blood around your body.

heavy adjective **heavier, heaviest**
Something that is heavy is hard to lift or carry because it weighs a lot.

hedge noun **hedges**
A hedge is a kind of wall made by bushes growing close together.

held See **hold**.
Mum held my hand tightly.

helicopter noun **helicopters**
A helicopter is a small aircraft without wings. It has large blades that spin round on top. It can fly straight up from the ground and hover in the air.

help verb **helps, helping, helped**
When you help somebody, you do something useful for them. *Can you help me with my homework?*

hen noun **hens**
A hen is a female chicken.

hid See **hide**.
I hid behind a tree while Max was counting to twenty.

hidden See **hide**.
Sophie has hidden my shoes and I can't find them.

a b c d e f g h i j k l m n o p q r s t u v w x y z

hide verb **hides, hiding, hid, hidden**
1 When you hide, you get into a place where no one can see you.
2 If you hide something, you put it into a place where no one can see it.

high adjective **higher, highest**
1 Something like a wall or a mountain that is high goes up a long way.
2 If something is high in the air, it is a long way up. *I threw a ball high into the air.*

hill noun **hills**
A hill is land that is higher than the land around it. Hills are smaller than mountains.

history noun
History is learning about what happened in the past.

hit verb **hits, hitting, hit**
If you hit something, you touch it hard. *I hit the ball over the fence with a bat.*

hive noun **hives**
A hive is a kind of box for keeping bees in.

hold verb **holds, holding, held**
1 If you hold something, you have it in your hands or arms. *Can I hold the baby?*
2 To hold means to have room inside for something. *This case will hold all my pencils.*

hole noun **holes**
A hole is a gap or opening in something. *There's a hole in my sock.*

holiday noun **holidays**
A holiday is time off from school or work.

hollow adjective
Something hollow has an empty space inside it.

home noun **homes**
A person's home is the place where they live.

honey noun
Honey is a sweet, sticky food made by bees.

hoof noun **hoofs** or **hooves**
A hoof is the hard part of a horse's foot. Cows and deer have hoofs, too.

hop verb **hops, hopping, hopped**
When you hop, you jump on one leg. Some animals and birds hop on two legs together.

a b c d e f g h i j k l m n o p q r s t u v w x y z

hope verb **hopes, hoping, hoped**
When you hope that something is going to happen, you want it to happen.
I hope you get better soon.

horn noun **horns**
A horn is a kind of pointed bone that grows out of the heads of cows and other animals.

horse noun **horses**
A horse is an animal with hoofs that is used for riding and pulling carts.

hospital noun **hospitals**
A hospital is a place where people who are ill or hurt are looked after.

hot adjective **hotter, hottest**
1 When something is hot, it burns you if you touch it.
2 If you feel hot, you are too warm.

house noun **houses**
A house is a building where people live.

hover verb **hovers, hovering, hovered**
If something hovers, it stays in one place in the air.

hug verb **hugs, hugging, hugged**
If you hug someone, you put your arms around them and hold them tightly.

huge adjective
Something huge is very big.

human noun **humans**
A human is a man, woman, or child.

hung See **hang**.
Yasmin hung her coat on the hook.

hungry adjective **hungrier, hungriest**
If you are hungry, you want something to eat.

hunt verb **hunts, hunting, hunted**
1 To hunt means to go after a wild animal to kill it. *Owls hunt at night.*
2 When you hunt for something, you look carefully for it. *I've hunted everywhere for my pen but I cannot find it.*

hurry verb **hurries, hurrying, hurried**
When you hurry, you move or do something quickly. *Let's hurry or we'll be late.*

hurt verb **hurts, hurting, hurt**
When something hurts, you feel pain there.
My knee really hurts.

hutch noun **hutches**
A hutch is a kind of cage for a pet rabbit.

a b c d e f g h **i** j k l m n o p q r s t u v w x y z

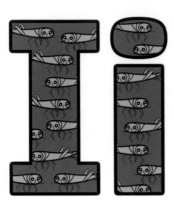

ice noun
Ice is water that has frozen hard.

ice cream noun **ice creams**
Ice cream is a sweet, frozen food made from milk or cream.

icicle noun **icicles**
An icicle is a hanging piece of ice made from dripping water that has frozen hard.

idea noun **ideas**
An idea is something that you have thought of. *I've got a great idea for a story.*

ill adjective
Someone who is ill does not feel well.

illness noun **illnesses**
If you have an illness, you do not feel well.

imagine verb **imagines, imagining, imagined**
If you imagine something, you make a picture of it in your mind. *Imagine you are a giant.*

immediately
If you do something immediately, you do it at once.

important adjective
1 If something is important, it matters a lot or is worth thinking about.
2 If someone is important, people take a lot of notice of what that person says and does.

impossible adjective
If something is impossible, it cannot be done.

information noun
Information is facts that tell people about something. *I need some information about dolphins and whales.*

ink noun
Ink is the coloured liquid that is used for writing with a pen.

insect noun **insects**
An insect is a very small creature with six legs. Flies, ants, grasshoppers, and bees are all insects.

instructions noun

Instructions are words and pictures that tell people what to do. *There are instructions for playing the game on the lid of the box.*

instrument noun **instruments**

1 Instruments are things that help you do a special job. *My dentist has a lot of instruments.*

2 An instrument is also something that you can use to make music.

interesting adjective

If something is interesting, you want to spend time on it or want to learn more about it.

interrupt verb **interrupts, interrupting, interrupted**

If you interrupt somebody, you stop them in the middle of what they are saying or doing.

invent verb **invents, inventing, invented**

If you invent something new, you are the first person who thinks of how to make it. *My uncle is inventing a drink that will make you invisible.*

invisible adjective

Things that are invisible cannot be seen.

invite verb **invites, inviting, invited**

If you invite someone to a party, you ask them to come to it.

iron noun **irons**

1 Iron is a strong, heavy metal.

2 An iron is a hot tool that you use to make clothes smooth and flat.

island noun **islands**

An island is a piece of land with water all round it.

a
b
c
d
e
f
g
h
i
j
k
l
m
n
o
p
q
r
s
t
u
v
w
x
y
z

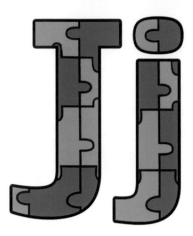

jacket noun jackets
A jacket is a short coat.

jam ❶ noun jams
1 Jam is a food that is made by boiling fruit with sugar until it is thick.
2 A traffic jam is a lot of cars crowded together so that nothing can move.

jam ❷ verb jams, jamming, jammed
If something jams, it becomes stuck and difficult to move. *This drawer has jammed and won't open.*

jar noun jars
Jars are usually made of glass. They hold things like jam.

jet noun jets
A jet is a very fast aeroplane.

jewel noun jewels
A jewel is a valuable and beautiful stone.

jigsaw noun jigsaws
A jigsaw is a puzzle made from a picture. When you fit the pieces together properly, you can see the picture.

job noun jobs
1 Someone's job is the work that they do to earn money.
2 A job is also something you have to do. *My job is to tidy my room every week.*

join verb joins, joining, joined
If you join two things, you put them together. *Join the dots to make a picture.*

joke noun jokes
A joke is a short story or a riddle that makes people laugh.

journey noun journeys
A journey is the travelling that people do to get from one place to another.

jug noun jugs
A jug is used for holding and pouring liquids. It has a handle and a spout.

juice noun juices
Juice is the liquid that comes out of fruit.

jump verb jumps, jumping, jumped
When you jump, you go suddenly into the air with both feet off the ground. *Ron jumped high in the air.*

jumper noun jumpers
A jumper is a piece of clothing with long sleeves that you wear on the top part of your body.

jungle noun jungles
A jungle is a thick forest in a warm, wet part of the world.

Kk

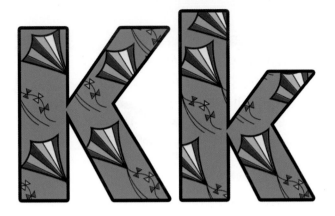

kangaroo noun **kangaroos**

A kangaroo is a large, Australian animal with strong back legs that it uses for jumping. A female kangaroo has a pocket at the front, where it carries its baby.

keep verb **keeps, keeping, kept**

1 If you keep something, you have it as your own and do not give it away. *Do you want to keep your old toys?*

2 If you keep an animal, you look after it. *My grandma keeps chickens.*

3 To keep also means to make something stay as it is. *Sid blew on his hands to keep them warm.*

kennel noun **kennels**

A kennel is a little house for a dog to sleep in.

kept See **keep**.

The noise kept us awake all night.

kettle noun **kettles**

A kettle is used to boil water in. It has a handle and a spout.

key noun **keys**

1 A key is a piece of metal shaped so that it fits into a lock.

2 A key is also a small bar or button that you press with your finger. Pianos and computers have keys.

kick verb **kicks, kicking, kicked**

When you kick, you hit something with your foot.

kill verb **kills, killing, killed**

To kill means to make someone or something die.

kind ❶ adjective **kinder, kindest**

Someone who is kind is ready to help other people. *It was very kind of you to let us play in your garden.*

kind ❷ noun **kinds**

If things are of the same kind, they belong to the same group. *A drum is a kind of instrument.*

king noun **kings**

A king is a man who has been born to rule a country.

a b c d e f g h i j k l m n o p q r s t u v w x y z

53

a b c d e f g h i j k l m n o p q r s t u v w x y z

kiss verb **kisses, kissing, kissed**
When you kiss someone, you touch them with your lips.
I kissed Mum and Dad goodnight.

kitchen noun **kitchens**
A kitchen is a room where food is cooked.

kite noun **kites**
A kite is a light toy that you can fly in the wind at the end of a long piece of string.

kitten noun **kittens**
A kitten is a very young cat.

knee noun **knees**
Your knee is the bony part in the middle of your leg where it bends.

kneel verb **kneels, kneeling, knelt**
When you kneel, you get down on your knees.

knelt See **kneel**.
Steven knelt down to play with the cat.

knew See **know**.
I knew the answer to the riddle.

knife noun **knives**
A knife is a tool with a long, sharp edge for cutting things.

knock verb **knocks, knocking, knocked**
When you knock something, you hit it hard. *I knocked my head on the shelf. Someone is knocking on the door.*

knot noun **knots**
A knot is the twisted part where two pieces of string or rope have been tied together.

know verb **knows, knowing, knew, known**
1 When you know something, you have found it out and you have it in your mind. *I know the answer to that question.*
2 If you know somebody, you have met them before. *I know that boy. He lives in our street.*

known See **know**.
I've known Ahmed for ages.

label noun **labels**
A label tells you something about the thing that it is fixed on to. Labels on clothes tell you what they are made of, and how to clean them.

lace noun **laces**
1 A lace is a piece of thin cord that is used to tie up a shoe.
2 Lace is a material with a pattern of small holes in it. It is often used to decorate things.

ladder noun **ladders**
A ladder is two long bars with short bars between them. People use ladders for climbing up and down.

lady noun **ladies**
Lady is a polite word for a woman.

ladybird noun **ladybirds**
A ladybird is a small flying beetle. Most ladybirds are red with black spots.

laid See **lay** ❶.
Has anyone laid the table?

lain See **lie** ❶.
Alex has lain in bed all day.

lake noun **lakes**
A lake is a lot of water with land all round it.

lamb noun **lambs**
A lamb is a young sheep.

lamp noun **lamps**
A lamp gives light where you want it.

land ❶ noun
Land is all the parts of the earth's surface that are not covered with water.

land ❷ verb **lands, landing, landed**
When people land, they arrive by aeroplane or boat.

lane noun **lanes**
1 A lane is a narrow country road.
2 Wide roads are also divided up into strips called lanes.

language noun **languages**
Language is the words that people use to speak or write to each other. There are many different languages spoken in the world. *This dictionary is written in the English language.*

a
b
c
d
e
f
g
h
i
j
k
l
m
n
o
p
q
r
s
t
u
v
w
x
y
z

a b c d e f g h i j k l m n o p q r s t u v w x y z

lap ❶ noun **laps**
When you are sitting down, your lap is the part from the top of your legs to your knees.

lap ❷ verb **laps, lapping, lapped**
When an animal laps, it drinks using its tongue. *Our kitten lapped up the milk from the bowl.*

large adjective **larger, largest**
If a thing is large, it is bigger than other things. *Can I have a large bag of popcorn?*

last
If you are last, you come after all the others. *I came last in the race.*

late adjective **later, latest**
1 If you are late, you arrive after the proper time.
2 Late also means near the end of a time. *These flowers will come up in late spring.*

laugh verb **laughs, laughing, laughed**
When you laugh, you make sounds to show you are happy or think something is funny.

law noun **laws**
A law is a rule that everyone in a country must keep.

lawn noun **lawns**
A lawn is the part of a garden that is covered with short grass.

lay ❶ verb **lays, laying, laid**
1 If you lay something down, you put it down carefully.
2 When you lay a table, you get it ready for a meal.
3 When a bird lays an egg, the egg comes out of the bird's body.

lay ❷ See **lie**.
We lay on the grass, looking up at the clouds.

layer noun **layers**
A layer is something flat that lies over or under another surface.
The cake had three layers of chocolate icing and a topping too.

lazy adjective **lazier, laziest**
Lazy people do not like working.

lead ❶ verb **leads, leading, led**
1 If you lead people, you go in front of them to show them where to go or what to do.
2 If you are leading in a race or game, you are winning it.
3 To lead also means to be in charge of a group.

lead ❷ noun **leads**
A lead is a strap fixed to a dog's collar so that you can control it.

lead ❸ noun
Lead is a soft, grey metal that is very heavy.

leader noun **leaders**
A leader is a person or animal that is in charge of a group.

leaf noun **leaves**
A leaf is one of the flat parts that grow on plants and trees. Most leaves are green.

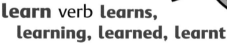

learn verb **learns, learning, learned, learnt**
When you learn, you get to know something you did not know before. *I am taking lessons to learn how to play the piano.*

leather noun
Leather is a strong material made from the skins of animals. It is used to make things like bags, gloves, and shoes.

leave verb **leaves, leaving, left**
1 If you leave, you go away from a place. *What time do you leave school?*
2 If you leave something somewhere, you let it stay where it is. *You can leave your bag here.*

led See **lead ❶**.
2 *Kim led the race from beginning to end.*

left ❶ noun
Left is the side that is opposite to the right.

left ❷ See **leave**.
2 *I left my coat on the bus.*

leg noun **legs**
1 Legs are the parts of the body that a person or animal uses for walking.
2 The legs of a table or chair are the parts that touch the floor.

lend verb **lends, lending, lent**
When somebody lends you something, they let you have it for a short time and you promise to give it back later. *Please could you lend me your red pen?*

length noun **lengths**
The length of something is how long it is. *How would you measure the length of a giraffe's neck?*

less
Less means not as much. *There is less water in a pond than in a lake.*

lesson noun **lessons**
A lesson is the time when someone is teaching you something.

let verb **lets, letting, let**
If someone lets you do something, they say you may do it. *Please let me use the computer.*

letter noun letters
1 A letter is one of the signs used for writing words. A, b, c, and d are letters. There are 26 letters in the alphabet.
2 A letter is also a message that you write to someone.

Dear Sarah,
Thanks for inviting me to your party.
From Amina.

lever noun levers
A lever is a bar that you pull down to lift or open something, or to make a machine work.

library noun libraries
A library is a place where a lot of books are kept. You can go to read them there or borrow them to read at home.

lick verb licks, licking, licked
When you lick something, you move your tongue over it.

To Sarah

lid noun lids
A lid is a top or cover for something like a box or a jar.

lie ❶ noun lies
A lie is something you say that you know is not true.

lie ❷ verb lies, lying, lay, lain
If you lie, you rest with your body flat. *Tom was lying on the grass looking at clouds.*

lifeboat noun lifeboats
A lifeboat is a boat that goes out to sea to rescue people who are in danger.

lift verb lifts, lifting, lifted
If you lift something, you pick it up and move it upwards.

light ❶ noun lights
Light is what lets you see. It comes from the sun, flames, and lamps.

light ❷ verb lights, lighting, lit
If you light something, you start it burning. *Dad is going to light the fire.*

light ❸ adjective lighter, lightest
1 Things that are light are easy to lift or carry. *Feathers are very light.*
2 Colours that are light are pale. *I have some light blue jeans.*

lightning noun
Lightning is the bright light that flashes in the sky when there is a thunderstorm.

a b c d e f g h i j k l m n o p q r s t u v w x y z

like ➊
Something that is like something else is nearly the same. *That girl has a hat like mine.*

like ➋ verb **likes, liking, liked**
If you like somebody or something, you think they are nice. *I like football very much.*

line noun **lines**
1 A line is a long, thin mark. *Write your name on the line.*
2 A line is also a row of people or things.
3 A railway line is the set of metal rails that a train moves on.

lion noun **lions**
A lion is a large wild cat. A male lion has a circle of long fur around its head.

lip noun **lips**
Your lips are the outside edges of your mouth.

liquid noun **liquids**
A liquid is anything that pours easily, like water, milk, or oil.

list noun **lists**
A list is a group of things or names that you write down one after the other.

listen verb **listens, listening, listened**
When you listen, you pay attention so that you can hear something. *Anissa is in her bedroom, listening to a CD.*

lit See **light** ➋.
It was cold, so we lit the fire.

litter noun **litters**
1 Litter is paper, empty packets, bottles, and other rubbish that people drop or leave behind.
2 A litter is all the young animals born to the same mother at the same time.

little adjective **littler, littlest**
1 If something is little, it is smaller than other things like it.
2 A little period of time does not last very long. *We'll be home in a little while.*
3 A little means not very much. *There's only a little juice left.*

live verb **lives, living, lived**
1 If something is living, it is alive.
2 If you live in a place, that is where your home is.

lizard noun **lizards**
A lizard is a reptile with a long body, four legs, and a long tail.

a
b
c
d
e
f
g
h
i
j
k
l
m
n
o
p
q
r
s
t
u
v
w
x
y
z

59

load noun **loads**
A load is a lot of heavy things to carry. *The lorry was carrying a load of rocks.*

lock noun **locks**
A lock is used to keep things like doors or cases shut. You cannot open a lock without the right key.

lolly noun **lollies**
A lolly is a hard sweet on a stick or a piece of fruity ice on a stick.

long adjective **longer, longest**
1 Something that is long measures a lot from one end to the other. *An elephant has a long trunk.*
2 Something that is long takes a lot of time. *This is a very long film.*

look verb **looks, looking, looked**
1 When you look, you use your eyes. *Look at the fire engine.*
2 If you look for something, you try to find it. *I've looked everywhere for my gloves.*

loose adjective **looser, loosest**
If something is loose, it is not fixed firmly. *One of these wheels is loose.*

lorry noun **lorries**
A lorry is a big, open truck for taking heavy things by road.

lose verb **loses, losing, lost**
1 If you lose something, you cannot find it. *I keep losing my pen.*
2 If you lose in a game or race, someone beats you.

lost ❶ See **lose**.
1 *I have lost one of my shoes.*

lost ❷ adjective
If you are lost, you do not know where you are. *We got lost in the fog.*

lot noun **lots**
A lot is a large number or amount. *There are a lot of shells on this beach.*

loud adjective **louder, loudest**
Something loud is easy to hear.

love verb **loves, loving, loved**
If you love someone, you like them very much.

lovely adjective **lovelier, loveliest**
Something lovely is enjoyable or beautiful.

low adjective **lower, lowest**
If something is low, it is close to the ground.

lucky adjective **luckier, luckiest**
If someone is lucky, good things seem to happen to them.

lunch noun **lunches**
Lunch is the meal that people eat in the middle of the day.

lying See **lie** ❷.
That dog has been lying in front of the fire all day.

Mm

machine noun **machines**
A machine has parts that work together to do a job.

made See **make**.
We made a tree house in the garden.

magazine noun **magazines**
A magazine is a kind of thin book that comes out every week or month. It has stories and pictures in it.

magic noun
1 In stories, people use magic to do impossible things.
2 Magic is also doing clever tricks that seem to be impossible. *I did a magic trick with three cups and a ball.*

magnet noun **magnets**
A magnet is a piece of metal that can make pieces of iron or steel stick to it.

main adjective
Main means the most important or the biggest. *We have our main meal of the day in the evening.*

make verb **makes, making, made**
1 If you make something, you get something new by putting other things together. *Mum said she'd help me make a cake.*
2 If you make a thing happen, it happens because of something you have said or done. *Our grandfather's jokes always make us laugh.*

male noun **males**
A male is any person or animal that belongs to the sex that cannot have babies. Boys and men are males.

mammal noun **mammals**
A mammal is an animal that can feed its babies with its own milk. Dogs, cows, whales, and people are all mammals.

man noun **men**
A man is a fully grown male person.

manage verb **manages, managing, managed**
If you can manage, you can do something although it is difficult.

many
Many means a lot of something. *There are many stars in the sky.*

map noun **maps**
A map is a drawing of part of the world. Maps tell you where different places are and show you things like towns, roads, rivers, and mountains.

mark noun **marks**
A mark is a spot or line on a surface that spoils it.

a
b
c
d
e
f
g
h
i
j
k
l
m
n
o
p
q
r
s
t
u
v
w
x
y
z

61

marmalade noun

Marmalade is a jam made from oranges or lemons.

marry verb **marries, marrying, married**

When two people marry, they become husband and wife.

mask noun **masks**

A mask is a cover that you can wear over your face. People wear masks to protect their faces or to change the way they look.

mat noun **mats**

A mat is a piece of thick material that covers part of the floor.

match ❶ noun **matches**

1 A match is a small, thin stick that makes a flame when it is rubbed on something rough.
2 A match is also a game played between two people or teams.

match ❷ verb **matches, matching, matched**

If one thing matches another, it is like it in some way. *In this card game you need to find the cards that match.*

material noun **materials**

1 A material is anything that can be used to make something else. Wood, stone, and plastic are materials.

2 Material is something that you can use to make things like clothes and curtains.

matter verb **matters, mattering, mattered**

If something matters, it is important. *It doesn't matter if we are a bit late.*

meadow noun **meadows**

A meadow is a field in the country that is covered with grass.

meal noun **meals**

A meal is the food that you eat at one go at breakfast, lunch, dinner or tea.

mean ❶ adjective **meaner, meanest**

1 If something you do is mean, it is not kind to someone else. *It is mean to tease your little brother.*
2 Someone who is mean does not like spending money or sharing things.

mean ❷ verb **means, meaning, meant**

1 If someone tells you what a word means, they tell you how to use it. *Do you know what the word bargain means?*
2 If you mean to do something, you plan to do it. *I'm sorry – I didn't mean to hurt you.*

meant See **mean ❷**.

2 *I meant to tell you, but I forgot.*

measles noun

Measles is an illness that makes you have red spots on your skin.

a b c d e f g h i j k l m n o p q r s t u v w x y z

measure verb **measures, measuring, measured**
When you measure something, you find out how big it is. *I used a height chart to measure how tall I was.*

meat noun
Meat is food that comes from animals that have been killed.

medicine noun **medicines**
Medicine is a liquid or pills that a sick person takes to help them get better.

meet verb **meets, meeting, met**
When people meet, they come together. *We'll meet you outside the cinema.*

melt verb **melts, melting, melted**
When something melts, it turns into a liquid as it gets hotter.

mend verb **mends, mending, mended**
When you mend something that is damaged, you make it useful again. *Mum, can you help me mend my bike?*

mess noun
If something is in a mess, it is untidy or dirty.

message noun **messages**
You send a message when you want to tell someone something and you cannot speak to them yourself.

messy adjective **messier, messiest**
If something is messy, it is untidy or dirty.

met See **meet**.
We met my uncle and aunt at the railway station.

metal noun **metals**
Metal is a hard material that melts when it is very hot. Gold, silver, and iron are all kinds of metal.

mice See **mouse**.

microwave noun **microwaves**
A microwave is a kind of oven that heats or cooks food very quickly.

middle noun
The middle of something is the part that is the same distance from all its sides. *Draw a heart in the middle of the paper.*

midnight noun
Midnight is twelve o'clock at night.

might verb
If something might happen, it is possible it will happen. *It might rain tomorrow.*

milk noun
Milk is a white liquid that mothers and female mammals feed their babies with. People often drink cows' milk.

mind ❶ noun **minds**
Your mind is the part of you that thinks, feels, understands, and remembers.

a b c d e f g h i j k l **m** n o p q r s t u v w x y z

mind ❷ verb **minds, minding, minded**
1 If you mind about something, you are worried or bothered by it. *Do you mind if I open the window?*
2 If you mind something or somebody, you look after them for a short time. *Please mind the baby while I go next door.*
3 If someone tells you to mind something, they want you to be careful. *Mind that broken glass.*

mirror noun **mirrors**
A mirror is a piece of glass that you can see yourself in.

miss verb **misses, missing, missed**
1 If you try to hit something and you miss, you do not hit it.
2 If you miss a bus or train, you do not catch it.
3 If you miss somebody, you feel sad because they are not there with you.

mistake noun **mistakes**
A mistake is something that you did not get right.

mix verb **mixes, mixing, mixed**
When you mix things, you stir or shake them until they become one thing.

mixture noun **mixtures**
A mixture is made of different things mixed together.

model noun **models**
A model is a small copy of something.

mole adjective **moles**
A mole is a small, furry animal that digs tunnels under the ground.

moment noun **moments**
A moment is a very small amount of time. *Wait here – I'll only be a moment.*

money noun
Money is the coins and paper notes that people use to buy things.

monkey noun **monkeys**
A monkey is an animal that lives in the trees in hot countries. It swings and climbs using its hands, feet, and long tail.

monster noun **monsters**
In stories, a monster is a huge, horrible creature.

month noun **months**
A month is part of a year. There are twelve months in a year.

moon noun **moons**
The moon moves round the Earth once every twenty-eight days. You can often see the moon shining in the sky at night.

more
More means a larger amount of something. *There is more water in a lake than in a pond.*

morning noun
mornings
The morning is the
time from the beginning
of the day until twelve o'clock noon.
The sun rises in the morning.

mother noun mothers
A mother is a woman who has a son or
a daughter.

motorbike noun
motorbikes
A motorbike is a
kind of heavy bicycle with an engine.

motorway noun motorways
A motorway is a very wide road, made
so that traffic can move fast.

mountain noun mountains
A mountain is a very high hill.

mouse noun mice
1 A mouse is a very small
animal with a long tail
and a pointed nose.
2 A mouse is also a small
box with buttons that you press to move
things around on a computer screen.

mouth noun mouths
Your mouth is the part of your face that
you open for speaking and eating.

move verb moves, moving, moved
1 If you move, you go from one place
to another. *Let's move into the shade.*
2 If you move something, you take it from
one place to another. *Please move your
toys off the floor.*

much
Much means a lot of something. *I don't
want much rice.*

mud noun
Mud is wet earth.

mug noun mugs
A mug is a large cup that does not need
a saucer.

multiply verb multiplies, multiplying, multiplied
When you multiply, you find the answer
to a sum like

$$2 \times 3 = 6$$

mum noun mums
Mum or mummy is what you call your
mother.

muscle noun muscles
Muscles are the parts inside your body
that help you move.

museum noun museums
A museum is a place where a lot of
interesting things are kept for people to
go and see.

mushroom noun mushrooms
A mushroom is a living thing that grows in
the earth and looks like a little umbrella.

music noun
Music is the sounds that are made by
someone singing, or playing a
musical instrument.

Nn

nail noun **nails**
1 A nail is the hard part that covers the end of each finger and toe.
2 A nail is also a small piece of metal with a sharp point. Nails are used to join pieces of wood together.

name noun **names**
A name is what you call someone or something.

narrow adjective **narrower, narrowest**
Something that is narrow does not measure very much from one side to the other.

nasty adjective **nastier, nastiest**
1 Something that is nasty is not at all nice.
2 Someone who is nasty is not at all kind.

natural adjective
Something that is natural has not been made by people or machines. Wool is a natural material.

nature noun
Nature is everything in the world that has not been made by people.

naughty adjective **naughtier, naughtiest**
A naughty puppy is one who behaves badly.

near adjective **nearer, nearest**
If something is near it is not far away. *Can I sit near the window?*

nearly
Nearly means very close to something. *He's nearly tall enough to reach the shelf.*

neat adjective **neater, neatest**
If something is neat, it is tidy and not in a mess.

neck noun **necks**
Your neck is the part of your body that joins your head to your shoulders.

necklace noun **necklaces**
A necklace is a piece of jewellery that you wear round your neck.

need verb **needs, needing, needed**
1 If people need something, they cannot live and be healthy without it. *Everybody needs water to drink.*
2 If you need something, you cannot manage without it. *I need another sheet of paper to finish my story.*

a b c d e f g h i j k l m n o p q r s t u v w x y z

needle noun needles

1 A needle is a very thin, pointed piece of metal. Needles used for sewing have holes in them for the thread to go through.

2 A needle can also be a thin leaf. Pine trees have needles.

neighbour noun neighbours

A neighbour is someone who lives near to you.

nephew noun nephews

A person's nephew is the son of their brother or sister.

nervous adjective

1 If you are nervous, you feel afraid and excited because of something you have to do. *I felt nervous about being in the play.*

2 A person or animal that is nervous is easily frightened. *Don't go near the nest – the mother bird is very nervous.*

nest noun nests

A nest is a home made by birds, mice, and some other animals for their babies.

net noun nets

A net is made of string or thread tied together with spaces in between. Nets are used in games like football and basketball. They are also used to catch fish and other animals.

never

Never means not at any time.

new adjective newer, newest

1 Something that is new has just been bought or made. *I got a new bike for my birthday.*

2 New can mean different. *I'm starting at a new school tomorrow.*

news noun

News is information about what has just happened. *Have you heard the news? We won the match!*

newspaper noun newspapers

A newspaper is a number of large sheets of paper folded together, with the news printed on them. Most newspapers come out every day.

next

1 Next means the one coming after this one. *Please turn over to the next page.*

2 Next means the one nearest to you. *Look who's sitting at the next table.*

nice adjective nicer, nicest

If somebody or something is nice, you like them. *Our new teacher is very nice.*

niece noun nieces

A person's niece is the daughter of their brother or sister.

a b c d e f g h i j k l m **n** o p q r s t u v w x y z

a
b
c
d
e
f
g
h
i
j
k
l
m
n
o
p
q
r
s
t
u
v
w
x
y
z

night noun **nights**
Night is the time when it is dark, after the sun goes down.

nightdress noun **nightdresses**
A nightdress is a kind of long, loose dress that girls and women wear in bed.

nightmare noun **nightmares**
A nightmare is a frightening dream.

nine noun **nines**
Nine is the number **9**.

nod verb **nods, nodding, nodded**
When you nod, you move your head down and then up again quickly, to show that you agree.

noise noun **noises**
A noise is a loud sound that someone or something makes. *The big truck made a lot of noise as it went by.*

noisy adjective **noisier, noisiest**
A lot of loud sound is noisy.

nonsense noun
Nonsense is something that someone says that is silly or does not mean anything.

noon noun
Noon is 12 o'clock in the middle of the day.

north noun
North is a direction. If you face towards the place where the sun comes up in the morning, north is on your left. **N** is north.

*N
W ← → E
S*

nose noun **noses**
Your nose is the part of your face that you use for breathing and smelling.

note noun **notes**
1 A note is a short letter.
2 A note is also one sound in music.

*Dear Amina
Thanks,
from Sarah.*

notice ❶ verb **notices, noticing, noticed**
If you notice something, you see it and think about it.

notice ❷ noun **notices**
A notice is a piece of paper or board that tells people something.

now
Now means at this time. *What time is it now?*

number noun **numbers**
Numbers tell you how many people or things there are. Numbers can be written as words (one, two, three), or as signs (1, 2, 3).

nurse noun **nurses**
A nurse is someone whose job is to take care of people who are ill or hurt.

nut noun **nuts**
A nut is a kind of dry fruit that you can eat after you have taken off its hard shell.

oar noun **oars**

An oar is a long pole with a flat part at one end. You use oars to row a boat.

obey verb **obeys, obeying, obeyed**

When you obey someone, you do what they tell you.

ocean noun **oceans**

An ocean is a very big sea.

octopus noun **octopuses**

An octopus is a sea animal with eight long arms and a soft body.

odd adjective **odder, oddest**

1 If something is odd, it seems strange.
2 An odd number cannot be divided by two without having something left over. 7, 13, and 27 are odd numbers.
3 Odd things do not belong in a pair. *Uncle David is wearing odd socks.*

offer verb **offers, offering, offered**

1 If you offer something, you ask someone if they would like it. *She offered me half her sandwich.*
2 If you offer to do something, you do not wait to be asked. *I offered to help wash up.*

often

If something happens often, it happens a lot.

oil noun

Oil is a thick, slippery liquid. It can be burned to keep people warm, or put on machines to help them move easily. Some kinds of oil are used in cooking.

old adjective **older, oldest**

1 Someone who is old was born a long time ago. *My grandfather is very old.*
2 Something that is old was made a long time ago. *This Greek vase is very old.*
3 You say something is old if you have had it a long time. *My old shoes are not as nice as my new ones.*

one noun

One is the number **1**.

open ❶

adjective
When something is open, people or things can go into it or through it. *Let's have the window, open.*

a
b
c
d
e
f
g
h
i
j
k
l
m
n
o
p
q
r
s
t
u
v
w
x
y
z

open ❷ verb **opens, opening, opened**
If you open something, you make it no longer shut or closed. *Open the door.*

opposite ❶ noun **opposites**
The opposite of something is the thing that is as different from it as possible. *Short is the opposite of tall.*

opposite ❷
If something is opposite something else, it is on the other side. *When you play chess, you sit opposite the other player.*

orange noun **oranges**
An orange is a round and sweet fruit with a thick peel.

orchestra noun **orchestras**
An orchestra is a large group of people playing musical instruments together.

order ❶ noun
Order is the way something is arranged. *The words in a dictionary are in alphabetical order.*

order ❷ verb **orders, ordering, ordered**
1 If someone orders you to do something, they say you have to do it. *The king ordered his men to attack.*
2 If you order something in a restaurant, you say that is what you want. *Mum ordered a chicken sandwich.*

ordinary adjective
Ordinary things are not special in any way. *To begin with, it was just an ordinary day.*

other
Other means not this one. *Where is my other shoe?*

outside
Outside means not inside a building. *Mum, please can I play outside?*

oven noun **ovens**
An oven is the space inside a cooker where food can be baked.

over
Over means above or on top of. *The car drove over the bridge.*

owe verb **owes, owing, owed**
If you owe money to someone, you have not yet paid them.

owl noun **owls**
An owl is a bird with a large, round head and large eyes. Owls hunt small animals at night.

own verb **owns, owning, owned**
1 If you own something, it is yours.
2 If you own up, you say that you were the one who did something.

paddle verb **paddles, paddling, paddled**
When you paddle, you walk about in water that is not very deep.

page noun **pages**
A page is one side of a piece of paper in a book.

pain noun **pains**
Pain is the feeling you have when part of your body hurts.

paint ❶ noun **paints**
Paint is a liquid that you put on the surface of something to colour it.

paint ❷ verb **paints, painting, painted**
1 If you paint a picture, you make a coloured picture with paints.
2 If someone paints something like a door, they put paint on to it.

painting noun **paintings**
A painting is a picture that someone has painted.

pair noun **pairs**
1 A pair is two people, two animals, or two things that belong together. *I bought Dad a pair of orange socks for his birthday.*
2 Things like trousers and scissors are also called a pair, because they have two parts joined together. *Have you got a pair of scissors?*

palace noun **palaces**
A palace is a very large, grand house where people like kings and queens live.

pale adjective **paler, palest**
Something that is pale in colour is almost white.

palm noun **palms**
Your palm is the inside of your hand between your fingers and your wrist.

panda noun **pandas**
A panda is a large animal with black and white fur that looks like bear.

pant verb **pants, panting, panted**
When a person or animal pants, they take short, quick breaths.

a b c d e f g h i j k l m n o p q r s t u v w x y z

71

a
b
c
d
e
f
g
h
i
j
k
l
m
n
o
p
q
r
s
t
u
v
w
x
y
z

pantomime noun **pantomimes**
A pantomime is a kind of play. It tells a fairy story, and has songs and jokes in it.

paper noun **papers**
1 Paper is a very thin material that is used for things like making books, and for writing on and for wrapping things up.
2 Paper is also short for newspaper.

parachute noun **parachutes**
A parachute is used to help people float slowly down to the ground after jumping out of an aeroplane. It is made of a large piece of material that looks like a huge umbrella.

parcel noun **parcels**
A parcel is something that is wrapped up so that it can be posted or given to someone as a present.

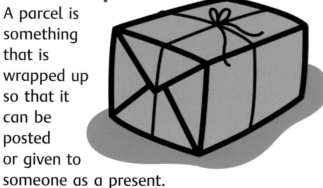

parent noun **parents**
Your parents are your mother and your father.

park ❶ noun **parks**
A park is a large piece of land with grass and trees where anyone can walk or play.

park ❷ verb **parks, parking, parked**
When people park a car, they leave it somewhere for a short time.

parrot noun **parrots**
A parrot is a bird with brightly coloured feathers and a large, curved beak.

part noun **parts**
A part is anything that belongs to something bigger. *A roof is part of a house.*

party noun **parties**
A party is when a group of people come together to enjoy themselves.

pass verb **passes, passing, passed**
1 If you pass something, you go by it. *I pass your school every day.*
2 If you pass something to someone, you give it to them with your hand.
3 If you pass a test, you do well. *My sister has passed her driving test.*

passenger noun **passengers**
A passenger is anyone travelling in a car, bus, train, ship, or aeroplane.

past noun
The past is the time before now.

pasta noun
Pasta is food made from flour, eggs, and water, that is made into shapes. You cook pasta in boiling water and eat it with sauce.

paste noun
Paste is a thick, wet mixture that you can use to stick paper to things.

pastry noun
Pastry is a mixture of flour, fat, and water which has been rolled and baked.

path noun **paths**
A path is a narrow way that you can go along.

patient ❶ adjective
If you are patient, you can wait for a long time, or do something difficult, without getting angry.

patient ❷ noun **patients**
A patient is someone who is ill and is being cared for by a doctor.

pattern noun **patterns**
A pattern is the way something is arranged, like lines and shapes on material, or sounds in music.

paw noun **paws**
A paw is an animal's foot.

pay verb **pays, paying, paid**
To pay means to give money for work or for things you have bought.

pebble noun **pebbles**
A pebble is a small, smooth stone you find on the beach.

pedal noun **pedals**
A pedal is a part that you press with your foot to make something work. A bicycle has two pedals.

peel noun
Peel is the skin on some fruit and vegetables.

pen noun **pens**
A pen is something you use to write with in ink.

pencil noun **pencils**
A pencil is a long, thin stick with black or a colour right through the middle. You use a pencil for writing or drawing.

penguin noun **penguins**
A penguin is a black and white bird that usually lives in very cold places. Penguins cannot fly but they are good swimmers.

people noun
People are men, women, and children.

pepper noun
Pepper is a powder that you add to food to give it a strong taste.

a b c d e f g h i j k l m n o p q r s t u v w x y z

73

a b c d e f g h i j k l m n o p q r s t u v w x y z

perch verb **perches, perching, perched**
When you perch on something, you sit on the edge of it, like a bird on a branch.

period noun **periods**
A period is a length of time.

person noun **people**
A person is a man, woman, or child.

pest noun **pests**
A pest is any person, animal, or plant that is a lot of trouble.

pet noun **pets**
A pet is a tame animal that you keep in your home. Cats and dogs are often kept as pets.

petal noun **petals**
A petal is a coloured part of a flower.

phone noun **phones**
Phone is short for telephone.

photo noun **photos**
A photo is a picture taken with a camera. Photo is short for photograph.

piano noun **pianos**
A piano is a large musical instrument. It has black and white keys that you press down with your fingers.

pick verb **picks, picking, picked**
1 If you pick somebody or something, you decide which one you want. *Salik picked three of his friends to be in his team.*
2 If you pick a thing up, you lift it.
3 If you pick flowers, fruit, or vegetables, you take them from where they are growing.

picnic noun **picnics**
A picnic is a meal you eat outdoors.

picture noun **pictures**
A picture is a painting, drawing, or photograph.

pie noun **pies**
A pie is meat or fruit covered with pastry and baked in an oven.

piece noun **pieces**
A piece of something is part of it. *The jigsaw has twelve pieces.*

pig noun **pigs**
A pig is an animal that is kept on a farm for its meat. Pigs have short, flat noses, called snouts, and curly tails.

pigeon noun **pigeons**
A pigeon is a bird with a fat body and a small head.

pile noun **piles**
A pile is a number of things put on top of one another.

pill noun **pills**
A pill is a small, round piece of medicine that can be swallowed whole.

pillow noun **pillows**
A pillow is something soft that you rest your head on in bed.

pilot noun **pilots**
A pilot is a person who flies an aeroplane.

pin noun **pins**
A pin is a short, thin piece of metal with a sharp point at one end. You use pins to hold pieces of paper or cloth together.

pipe noun **pipes**
A pipe is a long, thin tube that carries gas or water.

pirate noun **pirates**
A pirate is a sailor who attacks and robs other ships at sea.

pizza noun **pizzas**
A pizza is a large, flat pie covered with cheese, tomatoes, and other foods. You bake pizza quickly in a very hot oven.

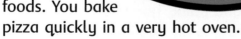

place noun **places**
A place is a particular part of a space or building. *Here's a good place for our picnic.*

plain adjective **plainer, plainest**
1 Something that is plain does not have a pattern on it.
2 If something is plain, it is easy to see or understand. *It is plain that you haven't been listening.*

plan verb **plans, planning, planned**
When you plan something, you decide what is going to be done. *Alex and Sarah are planning their magic show.*

plane noun **planes**
Plane is short for aeroplane.

planet noun **planets**
A planet is any of the worlds in space that move around a star. *The Earth, Mars, and Saturn are some of the planets which go around the Sun.*

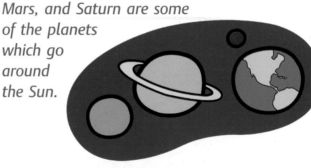

plant noun **plants**
A plant is anything that grows out of the ground. Trees, bushes, and flowers are all plants.

plaster noun **plasters**
1 A plaster is a sticky strip of material for covering cuts.
2 Plaster is a soft mixture that goes hard when it dries. Plaster is used to cover the walls inside buildings.

a b c d e f g h i j k l m n o p q r s t u v w x y z

a
b
c
d
e
f
g
h
i
j
k
l
m
n
o
p
q
r
s
t
u
v
w
x
y
z

plastic noun
Plastic is a light, strong material that is made in factories. It is used to make bottles, bowls, buckets, toys, and many other things.

plate noun **plates**
A plate is a flat dish that you put food on.

platform noun **platforms**
A platform in a station is the place where people wait for a train.

play verb **plays, playing, played**
1 When you play, you do something for fun. *Can we play in the garden?*
2 When you play a sport or game, you spend time trying to win it.
3 If you play a musical instrument, you make music with it.

playground noun **playgrounds**
A playground is a place outside where children can play.

please verb **pleases, pleasing, pleased**
1 If you are pleased about something, it makes you feel happy. *I was pleased to see my friend.*
2 You say please when you ask for something. *Please may I have some juice?*

plenty noun
If there is plenty of something, there is more than you need.

pocket noun **pockets**
A pocket is a small bag which is sewn into your clothes, for keeping things in.

poem noun **poems**
A poem is a piece of writing with a special rhythm. Poems usually have short lines and the words at the end of the lines often rhyme.

Roses are red
Violets are blue
Sugar is sweet
And so are you.

point ❶ noun **points**
1 A point is the sharp end of things like pins and pencils.
2 A point is also part of the score in a game.

point ❷ verb **points, pointing, pointed**
When you point, you show where something is by holding out your finger towards it.

pointed adjective
Something pointed has a sharp point at the end.

76

poisonous adjective
Poisonous things would make you ill or kill you if you swallowed them.

polar bear noun
polar bears
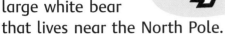
A polar bear is a large white bear that lives near the North Pole.

police noun
The police are the people whose job is to see that no one breaks the law.

polite adjective **politer, politest**
Someone who is polite is well behaved.

pond noun **ponds**
A pond is a small lake.

pony noun **ponies**
A pony is a small horse.

poor adjective **poorer, poorest**
1 Someone who is poor does not have much money.
2 Poor can also mean not very good. *It is difficult to read in this poor light.*

possible adjective
If something is possible, it can happen or be done.

post ❶ noun **posts**
1 A post is a tall, thick piece of wood or metal fixed in the ground.

2 The post is the letters or parcels that are delivered to your home. *Did my birthday card arrive in the post today?*

post ❷ verb **posts, posting, posted**
If you post something like a letter, you send it in the post.

poster noun **posters**
A poster is a large picture or notice for everyone to read.

potato noun **potatoes**
A potato is a vegetable that grows in the ground.

pour verb **pours, pouring, poured**
When you pour a liquid, you make it run out of something like a bottle or jug.
I poured myself a glass of orange.

powder noun **powders**
Powder is something that is made up of very tiny pieces, like dust or flour.

power noun
The power of something is the strength that it has. *This truck's engine has a lot of power.*

practise verb **practises, practising, practised**
When you practise something, you keep doing it so that you get better at it.

a
b
c
d
e
f
g
h
i
j
k
l
m
n
o
p
q
r
s
t
u
v
w
x
y
z

present ❶ noun **presents**

1 A present is something special you give to someone.

2 The present is the time right now.

present ❷ adjective

Someone who is present is in a particular place. *The mayor was present at the opening of the new school.*

president noun **presidents**

A president is someone who is chosen to lead a country.

press verb **presses, pressing, pressed**

When you press something, you push hard on it. *Tom pressed the button at the crossing.*

pretend verb **pretends, pretending, pretended**

When you pretend, you act as though something is true when it is not really. *Emma is pretending to be a ghost.*

pretty adjective **prettier, prettiest**

Pretty means nice to look at. *What pretty flowers!*

price noun **prices**

The price of something is how much money you have to pay to buy it.

prick verb **pricks, pricking, pricked**

If you prick something, you make a tiny hole with a sharp point.

prince noun **princes**

A prince is the son of a king or queen.

princess noun **princesses**

1 A princess is the daughter of a king or queen.

2 The wife of a prince is also called a princess.

prison noun **prisons**

A prison is a place where people are kept as a punishment for breaking the law.

prize noun **prizes**

A prize is something you get for winning or for doing something well.

problem noun **problems**

A problem is something that is hard to understand or to deal with.

programme noun **programmes**

1 A programme is a show on radio or television.

2 A programme is also a list that tells an audience what is going to happen.

project noun **projects**

When you do a project, you find out as much as you can about something and then write about it.

promise verb **promises, promising, promised**

When you promise, you say you will really do or not do something. *I promise I won't do it again.*

proper adjective

Proper means right. *I need the proper tool for this job.*

a b c d e f g h i j k l m n o p q r s t u v w x y z

protect verb **protects, protecting, protected**

If someone or something protects you, they keep you safe from harm. *You should wear a helmet to protect your head when you ride your bike.*

proud adjective **prouder, proudest**

If you feel proud, you are very pleased because you or someone close to you has done well. *I was proud of my brother when he won the race.*

pudding noun **puddings**

A pudding is something sweet like apple pie or trifle. You eat it at the end of a meal.

puddle noun **puddles**

A puddle is a small pool of water.

pull verb **pulls, pulling, pulled**

When you pull something, you get hold of it and make it come towards you.

puncture noun **punctures**

A puncture is a small hole in a tyre.

punishment noun **punishments**

A punishment is something that is done to someone who has done wrong.

pupil noun **pupils**

1 A pupil is someone who is being taught something.

2 Your pupils are the black spots in the middle of your eyes.

puppet noun **puppet**

A puppet is a kind of doll which can be made to move. Some puppets are put on like gloves, others are moved with strings from above.

puppy noun **puppies**

A puppy is a young dog.

pure adjective **purer, purest**

Something that is pure does not have anything else mixed with it. *Pure orange juice has no sugar or water added to it.*

purse noun **purses**

A purse is a small bag for carrying money.

push verb **pushes, pushing, pushed**

When you push something, you use your hands to move it away from you.

put verb **puts, putting, put**

When you put something somewhere, you move it there or leave it there. *Where did you put your coat?*

puzzle noun **puzzles**

A puzzle is a game or a question that is hard to work out.

pyjamas noun

Pyjamas are a pair of trousers and a loose jacket that you wear in bed.

a
b
c
d
e
f
g
h
i
j
k
l
m
n
o
p
q
r
s
t
u
v
w
x
y
z

quack verb **quacks, quacking, quacked**

When a duck quacks, it makes a noise through its beak.

quarrel verb **quarrels, quarrelling, quarrelled**

When people quarrel, they talk angrily and sometimes fight.

queen noun **queens**

1 A queen is a woman who was born to rule a country.
2 A king's wife is also called a queen.

question noun **questions**

A question is something you ask when you want to find something out.

queue noun **queues**

A queue is a line of people waiting for something.

quick adjective **quicker, quickest**

1 Something quick is done in a short time. *Let me have a quick look at your comic.*
2 To be quick means to move fast. *If we're quick, we'll be able to catch the bus.*

quiet adjective **quieter, quietest**

If someone or something is quiet, they make very little noise, or no noise at all.

quiz noun **quizzes**

A quiz is a kind of game or test. People try to answer questions to show how much they know.

rabbit noun **rabbits**
A rabbit is a small, furry animal with long ears. Rabbits live in holes in the ground.

race noun **races**
A race is a way of finding out who is the fastest.

radiator noun **radiators**
A radiator is made of metal, and is filled with hot water to heat a room.

radio noun **radios**
A radio is a machine that receives sounds sent through the air. You can listen to music, programmes, or messages on a radio.

rail noun **rails**
1 A rail is a bar joined to posts to make something like a fence.
2 A rail is also a long metal bar that is part of a railway line.

railway noun **railways**
A railway is a set of metal bars for trains to run on.

rain noun
Rain is water that falls from the sky in drops.

rainbow noun **rainbows**
A rainbow is the band of different colours that you can see in the sky when the sun shines through rain.

rainforest noun **rainforests**
A rainforest is a thick forest in a warm part of the world where a lot of rain falls.

ran See **run**.
When it started to rain, we ran home.

rang See **ring** ❷.
Melissa rang the doorbell.

a
b
c
d
e
f
g
h
i
j
k
l
m
n
o
p
q
r
s
t
u
v
w
x
y
z

81

rare adjective **rarer, rarest**
Something that is rare is not often found, or does not often happen. *Some animals are becoming very rare.*

rat noun **rats**
A rat looks like a mouse, but is larger.

rather
1 Rather means a little bit. *It's rather cold today.*
2 You say you would rather do something if you would like to do it more than something else. *I would rather watch the other television channel.*

raw adjective
Raw food is not cooked.

reach verb **reaches, reaching, reached**
1 To reach means to stretch out your hand to touch something. *If I stand on tiptoe I can just reach the book.*
2 To reach also means to arrive at a place. *We should reach London by evening.*

read verb **reads, reading, read**
When you read, you can understand words that are written down.

ready adjective
If you are ready, you can do something at once. *Are you ready to go?*

real adjective
1 Something that is real is not a copy. *Are those flowers real or made of paper?*
2 Real also means true and not made up. *Was Robin Hood a real person?*

really
Really means you are telling the truth, or you want to hear the truth. *Do you really have a pet snake?*

reason noun **reasons**
A reason explains why something happens or why you want to do something. *The reason I am late is that I missed the bus.*

receive verb **receives, receiving, received**
To receive means to get something that has been given or sent to you.

record ❶ noun **records**
A record is the best that has been done so far. *My record for getting dressed is two minutes.*

record ❷ verb **records, recording, recorded**
When you record something, you write it down or put it on tape or a CD. *Did you record that programme?*

recorder noun **recorders**
A recorder is a musical instrument. You play it by blowing into one end and covering holes with your fingers.

a b c d e f g h i j k l m n o p q r s t u v w x y z

reflection noun **reflections**

A reflection is what you see in a mirror, or in anything shiny.

refuse verb **refuses, refusing, refused**

If you refuse, you say you will not do something you have been asked to do.

remember verb **remembers, remembering, remembered**

To remember means to bring something back into your mind when you want to. *I can remember the names of all the planets.*

remind verb **reminds, reminding, reminded**

If you remind somebody of something, you help them to remember it.

remove verb **removes, removing, removed**

If you remove something, you take it away. *A rubber will remove pencil marks.*

repair verb **repairs, repairing, repaired**

When someone repairs something, they make it work properly again.

reply verb **replies, replying, replied**

When you reply, you give an answer. *Have you replied to Amy's party invitation?*

reptile noun **reptiles**

Reptiles are animals with cold blood. They have scaly skins, and short legs or no legs at all. Reptiles lay eggs.

rescue verb **rescues, rescuing, rescued**

If you rescue somebody, you save them from danger.

rest ❶ verb **rests, resting, rested**

When you rest, you lie down or sit quietly.

rest ❷ noun

The rest is the part that is left. *I've done most of my homework. I'll do the rest tomorrow.*

result noun **results**

A result is anything that happens because of other things. *We were late, and as a result we missed the bus.*

return verb **returns, returning, returned**

1 If you return, you go back to where you were before.

2 If you return something, you give it back.

a
b
c
d
e
f
g
h
i
j
k
l
m
n
o
p
q
r
s
t
u
v
w
x
y
z

a
b
c
d
e
f
g
h
i
j
k
l
m
n
o
p
q
r
s
t
u
v
w
x
y
z

reward noun **rewards**
A reward is given to you for something good that you have done.

rhinoceros noun **rhinoceroses**
A rhinoceros is a very large, heavy animal with thick skin. Rhinoceroses have one or two horns on their noses.

rhyme verb **rhymes, rhyming, rhymed**
Words that rhyme have the same sound at the end, like bat and cat.

rhythm noun **rhythms**
Rhythm is a repeated pattern of sounds in music or poetry.

ribbon noun **ribbons**
A ribbon is a thin strip of coloured material used to tie round hair or gifts.

rice noun
Rice is a white food that comes from the seeds of a kind of grass. Rice is the main food for many people in the world.

rich adjective **richer, richest**
People who are rich have a lot of money.

ridden See **ride**.
Have you ridden your new bike yet?

riddle noun **riddles**
A riddle is a kind of question that has a funny or clever answer.

ride verb **rides, riding, rode, ridden**
1 When you ride a bicycle or a horse, you sit on it as it goes along.
2 When you ride in something like a car or train, you travel in it.

right ❶ adjective
If something is right, there are no mistakes in it or it is as it should be.

right ❷ noun
Right is the side that is opposite the left.

ring ❶ noun **rings**
1 A ring is a circle. *The children sat in a ring around the storyteller.*
2 A ring can be a circle of thin metal that you wear on your finger.
3 A ring is also the sound a bell makes.

ring ❷ verb **rings, ringing, rang, rung**
When something rings, it makes the sound of a bell.

rise verb **rises, rising, rose, risen**
When something rises, it goes upwards. *When the sun rises it appears above the horizon.*

river noun **rivers**
A river is a lot of water that moves naturally and flows across the land to the sea or to a lake.

road noun **roads**
A road is a way between places, made for cars and buses, bicycles, and trucks.

roar verb **roars, roaring, roared**
To roar is to make a loud, deep sound, like a lion makes.

robot noun **robots**
A robot is a machine that can make some of the movements that a person can. In factories, robots can do some jobs that people find boring.

rock ❶ noun **rocks**
Rock is the hard, stony part of the earth. A rock is a piece of this.

rock ❷ verb **rocks, rocking, rocked**
If something rocks, it moves gently from side to side. *I hope the boat doesn't rock too much.*

rocket noun **rockets**
1 A rocket is part of a spacecraft. Hot gases rush from the end of the rocket and move the spacecraft upwards.
2 A rocket is also a kind of firework. When it is lit, it shoots high in the air.

rode See **ride**.
The queen rode a beautiful white horse.

roll noun **rolls**
1 A roll of something like tape or paper is a very long piece of it wrapped round and round lots of times.
2 A roll is also a small, round piece of bread made for one person.

roof noun **roofs**
A roof is the part that covers the top of a building or vehicle.

room noun **rooms**
A room is one of the spaces with walls round it in a building. A room has a floor, ceiling, and its own door.

root noun **roots**
A root is the part of a plant that grows under the ground.

rope noun **ropes**
Rope is a lot of strong threads twisted together.

rose ❶ noun **roses**
A rose is a flower with thorns on its stem. Roses often smell very nice.

rose ❷ See **rise**.
Black smoke rose from the bonfire.

rough adjective **rougher, roughest**
1 Something that is rough is not smooth.
2 If people are rough, they are not gentle.

a b c d e f g h i j k l m n o p q r s t u v w x y z

85

round ❶ adjective **rounder, roundest**
Round means shaped like a circle or a ball.

round ❷
Round means on all sides of something. *There is a wall round the garden.*

row ❶ noun **rows**
A row is a line of people or things.

row ❷ verb **rows, rowing, rowed**
When you row, you use oars to make a boat move through water.

rub verb **rubs, rubbing, rubbed**
If you rub something, you press your hand on it and move it backwards and forwards. *David rubbed his sore arm with his hand.*

rubber noun **rubbers**
1 Rubber is strong material that stretches, bends, and bounces. Rubber is used to make things like tyres and wellington boots.
2 A rubber is a small piece of soft rubber that you use to rub out pencil marks.

rubbish noun
Rubbish is things that are not wanted, like empty cans and waste paper.

rude adjective **ruder, rudest**
Someone who is rude behaves badly and is not polite.

ruin verb **ruins, ruining, ruined**
If you ruin something, you spoil it completely.

rule ❶ verb **rules, ruling, ruled**
Someone who rules is in charge of a country and the people who live there.

rule ❷ noun **rules**
Rules tell you what you can and cannot do. Games have rules, and places like schools have rules too.

ruler noun **rulers**
1 A ruler is a strip of wood or plastic used for measuring and drawing straight lines.

2 A ruler is also someone who rules a country.

run verb **runs, running, ran, run**
When you run, you use your legs to move quickly.

rung See **ring ❷**.
Have you rung the doorbell yet?

Ss

sad adjective **sadder, saddest**
If you are sad, you feel unhappy.

safe ❶ adjective **safer, safest**
If someone is safe, they are free from danger. *The cat felt safe up the tree.*

safe ❷ noun **safes**
A safe is a strong metal box where money or valuable things can be kept.

said See **say**.
Simon said he was sorry.

sail ❶ noun **sails**
A sail is a large piece of strong cloth joined to a boat. The wind blows into the sail and makes the boat move.

sail ❷ verb **sails, sailing, sailed**
To sail means to travel in a boat. *We sailed across the Atlantic.*

salad noun **salads**
Salad is a mixture of raw vegetables, usually eaten as part of a meal.

salt noun
Salt is a white powder you put on food to give it flavour.

same
If two things are the same, they are like each other in every way.

sand noun
Sand is powder made up of tiny bits of rock. Sand covers deserts and the land next to the sea.

sandal noun **sandals**
A sandal is an open shoe with straps that go over your foot. People wear sandals in warm weather.

sandwich noun **sandwiches**
A sandwich is two slices of bread with another food between them.

a b c d e f g h i j k l m n o p q r s t u v w x y z

a
b
c
d
e
f
g
h
i
j
k
l
m
n
o
p
q
r
s
t
u
v
w
x
y
z

sang See **sing**.
The mermaid sang a strange and beautiful song.

sank See **sink**.
There was a hole in the boat and it sank.

sari noun **saris**
A sari is a long piece of cloth which many Asian girls and women wear.

sat See **sit**.
Grandpa sat in an armchair by the fire.

saucepan noun **saucepans**
A saucepan is made of metal. It has a lid and a long handle. Saucepans are used to cook food.

saucer noun **saucers**
A saucer is a small plate for putting a cup on.

sausage noun **sausages**
A sausage is made of tiny pieces of meat mixed with herbs and put into a thin skin.

save verb **saves, saving, saved**
1 If you save something, you keep it so that you can use it later. *I'm saving money for a new football shirt.*
2 To save also means to keep someone or something safe from danger. *A helicopter saved two men whose boat had sunk.*

saw ❶ noun **saws**
A saw is a tool that has a blade with sharp teeth on one edge. Saws are used for cutting material like wood.

saw ❷ See **see**.
I saw you taking another chocolate from the box.

say verb **says, saying, said**
When you say something, you use your voice to make words.

scale noun **scales**
A scale is one of the small, thin pieces of hard skin that cover fish and reptiles.

scales noun
Scales are used to find out how heavy things are.

scared adjective
Someone who is scared feels afraid.

school noun **schools**
School is the place where children go to learn.

science noun **sciences**
Science is finding out about things that happen in the world around us. We do this by measuring things and by doing tests called experiments.

scissors noun
A pair of scissors is a tool for cutting paper or cloth. It has two sharp blades joined in the middle.

score ❶ verb **scores, scoring, scored**
To score means to get a goal or a point in a game.

score ❷ noun **scores**
The score is the number of points or goals each side has in a game.

scratch verb **scratches, scratching, scratched**
1 If you scratch something, you damage it by moving something sharp over it. *Be careful you don't scratch the table with those scissors.*
2 To scratch also means to move fingernails or claws over skin. *You scratched me!*

scream verb **screams, screaming, screamed**
If you scream, you cry out loudly, often because you are hurt or afraid.

screen noun **screens**
A screen is a smooth surface on which films or television programmes are shown. Computers have screens too.

sea noun **seas**
The sea is the salt water that covers most of the Earth's surface.

seal noun **seals**
A seal is a furry animal that lives in the sea and on land. Seals have flippers for swimming.

search verb **searches, searching, searched**
When you search, you look very carefully for something. *I've searched everywhere for my watch but I can't find it.*

a
b
c
d
e
f
g
h
i
j
k
l
m
n
o
p
q
r
s
t
u
v
w
x
y
z

a
b
c
d
e
f
g
h
i
j
k
l
m
n
o
p
q
r
s
t
u
v
w
x
y
z

seaside noun
> The seaside is a place beside the sea where people go for a holiday.

season noun **seasons**
> A season is one of the four parts of the year. The four seasons are called spring, summer, autumn, and winter.

seat noun **seats**
> A seat is anything that people sit on.

second
> If you are second, you are the next one after the first.

secret noun **secrets**
> A secret is something that you do not want other people to know about.

see verb **sees, seeing, saw, seen**
> When you see, you use your eyes to get to know something. *Can you see the balloon in the sky?*

seed noun **seeds**
> A seed is a tiny part of the fruit of a plant. When a seed is put in the ground, it can grow into a new plant.

seek verb **seeks, seeking, sought**
> If you seek something, you try to find it.

seem verb **seems, seeming, seemed**
> To seem means to appear or look a certain way. *You seem a bit quiet today.*

seen See **see**.
> *Have you seen my hamster anywhere?*

sell verb **sells, selling, sold**
> If someone sells you something, they let you have it for an amount of money.

send verb **sends, sending, sent**
> If you send a person or thing, you make them go somewhere. *I'm sending a card to Grandpa.*

sensible adjective
> Sensible people are good at knowing what is best to do.

sent See **send**.
> *Mum sent me to find you.*

serve verb **serves, serving, served**
> If someone serves you in a place like a shop or restaurant, they help you get what it is you want.

set ❶ noun **sets**
> A set is a group of things that belong together. *At school we use a geometry set.*

90

set ❷ verb **sets, setting, set**
1 When something sets, it becomes solid or hard.
2 When you set something somewhere, you put it down. *Jenny set the plates on the table.*

seven noun **sevens**
Seven is the number **7**.

sew verb **sews, sewing, sewed, sewn**
To sew means to use a needle and cotton to join pieces of cloth together, or to fix things on to cloth.

sewn See **sew**.
I've just sewn a badge on to my jacket.

sex noun **sexes**
The sexes are the two groups that all people and animals belong to. One group is male and the other is female.

shadow noun **shadows**
A shadow is the dark shape that is made by something standing in front of the light.

shake verb **shakes, shaking, shook, shaken**
1 When a thing shakes, it moves quickly up and down or from side to side. *The whole house shakes whenever a train goes past.*
2 If you shake something, you make it shake. *Shake the bottle before you pour the ketchup.*

shallow adjective **shallower, shallowest**
Something like water that is shallow is not deep. *I can stand up in the shallow end of the swimming pool.*

shape noun **shapes**
The shape of something is the pattern that its outside edges make. *Circles, squares, and triangles are all shapes.*

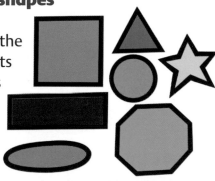

share verb **shares, sharing, shared**
If you share something, you make it into parts and give them to other people. *We shared the cake among the four of us.*

shark noun **sharks**
A shark is a large sea fish with lots of sharp teeth.

a b c d e f g h i j k l m n o p q r s t u v w x y z

sharp adjective **sharper, sharpest**
Something sharp has an edge or point that can cut or make holes.

shave verb **shaves, shaving, shaved**
When people shave, they cut hair from their skin to make it smooth.

shed noun **sheds**
A shed is a small wooden building. People often keep tools or bicycles in a shed.

sheep noun **sheep**
A sheep is an animal kept by farmers for its wool and meat.

sheet noun **sheets**
1 A sheet is one of the large pieces of cloth that you put on a bed.
2 A sheet is also a piece of paper or glass.

shelf noun **shelves**
A shelf is a long flat surface for putting things on. Bookcases and cupboards have shelves.

shell noun **shells**
A shell is the hard part on the outside of eggs, nuts, and some kinds of animals such as snails and tortoises.

shine verb **shines, shining, shone**
When something shines, it gives out light, or looks very bright. *The sun was shining and the sky was blue.*

shiny adjective **shinier, shiniest**
When things are shiny, they look very bright. *I cleaned the windows to make them shiny.*

ship noun **ships**
A ship is a large boat that takes people or things across the sea.

shirt noun **shirts**
You wear a shirt on the top half of your body. Shirts have sleeves, a collar, and buttons down the front.

shiver verb **shivers, shivering, shivered**
When you shiver, you shake because you are cold or frightened.

shoe noun **shoes**
A shoe is a strong covering for your foot.

shone See **shine**.
The sun shone all day.

92

shook See **shake**.
I shook my money box, but there was nothing in it.

shop noun **shops**
A shop is a place where people go to buy things.

short adjective **shorter, shortest**
1 A short distance or time is not very long. *It was a short walk to the shops.*
2 A short person is not very tall.

shorts noun
Shorts are short trousers that end above your knees.

shoulder noun **shoulders**
Your shoulder is the part of your body between your neck and the top of your arm.

shout verb **shouts, shouting, shouted**
When you shout, you speak very loudly. *Isabel shouted for help from the top of the tree.*

show ❶ verb **shows, showing, showed, shown**
1 When you show something, you let someone else see it. *Show me the picture you've done.*
2 If someone shows you how to do something, they do it so that you can watch them and learn how to do it. *Can you show me how to make a paper aeroplane?*

show ❷ noun **shows**
A show is something that is put on for you to watch, like a television programme, a play, or dancing.

shower noun **showers**
1 A shower is rain or snow that falls for only a short time.
2 A shower in the bathroom gives you a spray of water so that you can stand under it and wash all over.

shown See **show ❶**.
Have you shown Dan your hamsters?

shut verb **shuts, shutting, shut**
To shut means to move a cover, lid, or door to close up an opening. *Please shut the door behind you.*

shy adjective **shyer, shyest**
Someone who is shy is a bit nervous about talking to people they do not know.

sick adjective
Someone who is sick does not feel well. *Tara looked as though she was feeling sick.*

a
b
c
d
e
f
g
h
i
j
k
l
m
n
o
p
q
r
s
t
u
v
w
x
y
z

side noun **sides**

1 The side is the part that is on the left or right of something. *You start reading on the left side of the page in English.*

2 A side can be an edge. *A triangle has three sides.*

3 A side can also be a flat surface. *A cube has six sides.*

4 The two sides in a game are the groups playing against each other.

sign ❶ noun **signs**

A sign is anything that is written, drawn, or done to tell or show people something. *Did you see the sign for the park?*

sign ❷ verb **signs, signing, signed**

When you sign something, you write your name. *We can all sign Emma's birthday card.*

silent adjective

A person or thing that is silent does not make any sound at all.

silly adjective **sillier, silliest**

A silly person does something that is funny or not sensible.

silver noun

Silver is a valuable, shiny white metal.

sing verb **sings, singing, sang, sung**

When you sing, you make music with your voice.

sink ❶ noun **sinks**

A sink is a place where you can wash things.

sink ❷ verb **sinks, sinking, sank, sunk**

If something sinks, it goes downwards, usually under water.

sister noun **sisters**

Your sister is a girl who has the same parents as you do.

sit verb **sits, sitting, sat**

When you sit, you rest on your bottom on a chair or on the floor.

six noun **sixes**

Six is the number **6**.

size noun **sizes**

The size of something is how big it is.

skate noun **skates**

An ice skate is a special boot with a steel blade fixed underneath. A roller skate has small wheels instead.

skeleton noun **skeletons**
A skeleton is all the bones that hold up the body of a person or animal.

skin noun **skins**
1 Your skin is the outer covering of your body.
2 The outer covering of fruit and vegetables is also called skin.

skirt noun **skirts**
A skirt is worn by women and girls. It hangs down from the waist.

sky noun **skies**
The sky is the space above the Earth where you can see the clouds, sun, moon, and stars.

sleep verb **sleeps, sleeping, slept**
When you sleep, you close your eyes and let your body rest as it does every night.

sleeve noun **sleeves**
A sleeve is the part of something like a coat or shirt that covers your arm.

slept See **sleep**.
I slept in the little bedroom at the top of the house.

slice noun **slices**
A slice of something like bread or cake is a thin piece cut from the whole thing.

slide ❶ verb **slides, sliding, slid**
If you slide, you move smoothly over something slippery or polished.

slide ❷ noun **slides**
A slide is a smooth slope that you can slide down for fun.

slip verb **slips, slipping, slipped**
If you slip, you slide suddenly without meaning to.

slipper noun **slippers**
A slipper is a soft shoe that people wear indoors.

slippery adjective
Something slippery is so smooth or wet that it is difficult to get hold of or walk on.

slope noun **slopes**
A slope is ground that is like the side of a hill, with one end lower than the other. *The ball rolled away down the slope.*

slow adjective **slower, slowest**
Someone or something that is slow does not move very fast or takes a long time.

a
b
c
d
e
f
g
h
i
j
k
l
m
n
o
p
q
r
s
t
u
v
w
x
y
z

95

a
b
c
d
e
f
g
h
i
j
k
l
m
n
o
p
q
r
s
t
u
v
w
x
y
z

small adjective **smaller, smallest**
Small things are not as big as others of the same kind.

smash verb **smashes, smashing, smashed**
If something smashes, it breaks into lots of pieces with a loud noise.

smell verb **smells, smelling, smelt**
1 When you smell something, you use your nose to find out about it. *I can smell something burning.*
2 When something smells, you can find out about it with your nose. *That rose smells nice.*

smile verb **smiles, smiling, smiled**
When you smile, your face shows that you are feeling happy.

smoke noun
Smoke is a grey or black cloud of gas that floats up from a fire.

smooth adjective **smoother, smoothest**
Something that is smooth does not have any lumps or rough parts.

snail noun **snails**
A snail is a small, soft creature that lives inside a shell. Snails move very slowly.

snake noun **snakes**
A snake is a reptile with a long body and no legs. Some snakes can give poisonous bites.

sneeze verb **sneezes, sneezing, sneezed**
When you sneeze, you make a sudden noise as air rushes out of your nose.

snow noun
Snow is small, white pieces of frozen water. It floats down from the sky when the weather is very cold.

snowman noun **snowmen**
A snowman is a shape of a person made out of snow.

soap noun
You use soap with water for washing. Soap can be solid, liquid, or a powder.

sock noun **socks**
A sock is a soft covering for your foot and part of your leg.

sofa noun **sofas**
A sofa is a long comfortable seat with a back, for more than one person.

soft adjective **softer, softest**
Something that is soft is not hard or firm.

soil noun
Soil is the earth that plants grow in.

sold See **sell**.
Amy sold Tom her recorder.

soldier noun **soldiers**
A soldier is a person in an army.

solid adjective
1 Something that is solid does not have space inside. *This is a solid chocolate egg.*
2 Something that is solid does not change its shape. Liquids and gases are not solid, but rocks and metals are.

son noun **sons**
A person's son is their male child.

song noun **songs**
A song is words that are sung.

soon
Soon means in a short time. *I'll see you soon.*

sore adjective
sorer, sorest
Something that is sore feels painful.

sorry
You say you are sorry when you have done something wrong. *I'm sorry I forgot your birthday.*

sort ❶ noun **sorts**
If things are of the same sort, they belong to the same group or kind. *What sort of cake would you like?*

sort ❷ verb **sorts, sorting, sorted**
When you sort things, you arrange them into different groups.

sound noun **sounds**
A sound is anything you can hear. *I heard the sound of a dog barking.*

soup noun
Soup is a liquid food made from vegetables or meat and water. You eat soup with a spoon out of a bowl.

sour adjective
1 Things that are sour have the kind of taste a lemon or vinegar has.
2 If milk is sour, it is not fresh.

south noun
South is a direction.
S is south. If you look towards the place where the sun comes up in the morning, south is on your right.

space noun **spaces**
1 Space is an empty area where there is room for something. *Leave a space on the table for the cake.*
2 Space is everything beyond the Earth, where the stars and planets are.

spaceship noun **spaceships**
A spaceship is a vehicle that can carry people and things through space.

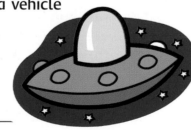

spade noun **spades**
A spade is a tool used for digging. It has a long handle and a short, wide blade.

speak verb **speaks, speaking, spoke, spoken**
If you speak, you say something.

a
b
c
d
e
f
g
h
i
j
k
l
m
n
o
p
q
r
s
t
u
v
w
x
y
z

97

a b c d e f g h i j k l m n o p q r s t u v w x y z

special adjective
1 If something is special, it is better than the usual kind. *Mum made a special cake for the party.*
2 Special also means made for a particular job. *You need special shoes for tap dancing.*

speed noun **speeds**
Speed is how quickly something moves or happens. *The car raced past at great speed.*

spell ❶ verb **spells, spelling, spelt, spelled**
When you spell a word, you say or write the letters in the right order. *H o r s e spells horse.*

spell ❷ noun **spells**
In stories, a spell is words that make magic things happen.

spend verb **spends, spending, spent**
1 When you spend money, you use it to pay for things.
2 When you spend time, you use it to do something. *I'd like to spend an hour writing some letters to my friends.*

spent See **spend**.
2 *We spent the weekend painting my room.*

spider noun **spiders**
A spider is a small creature with eight legs. Many spiders make webs to catch insects to eat.

spill verb **spills, spilling, spilt, spilled**
If you spill a liquid, you let it flow out when you did not mean to.

spin verb **spins, spinning, spun**
1 To spin means to turn round and round quickly. *The coin kept spinning on the table.*
2 To spin also means to make thread by twisting long, thin pieces of wool or cotton together.

spine noun **spines**
1 Your spine is the long row of bones down the middle of your back.
2 Spines are prickles or thorns on an animal or plant.

spire noun **spires**
A spire is a tall, pointed part of a church.

splash verb **splashes, splashing, splashed**
When liquid splashes, it flies about in drops. *The water splashed all over me.*

spoil verb **spoils, spoiling, spoilt, spoiled**
If something is spoilt, it is not as good as it was before. *The rain spoilt my new shoes.*

spoke See **speak**.
The old man spoke very softly.

spoken See **speak**.
Have you spoken to your new neighbours yet?

spoon noun **spoons**
You use a spoon to eat things like soup, cereal, and puddings.

sport noun **sports**
A sport is a game that you play to get exercise and have fun. Football, tennis, and swimming are sports.

spot noun **spots**
1 A spot is a round mark.
2 A spot is also a small, red bump on your skin.
3 A spot can mean a place. *Here's a good spot for a picnic.*

spout noun **spouts**
A spout is part of something like a teapot, kettle, or jug. It is made so that you can pour liquid out easily.

spring noun **springs**
1 Spring is the part of the year when plants start to grow and the days get longer and warmer.
2 A spring is a piece of metal that is wound into rings. It jumps back into shape after you press it down or stretch it.

spun See **spin**.
I spun round until I was dizzy.

square noun **squares**
A square is a shape with four corners and four sides that are the same length.

squirrel noun **squirrels**
A squirrel is a small wild animal with a long, bushy tail. Squirrels live in trees and eat nuts.

stable noun **stables**
A stable is a building where horses are kept.

stair noun **stairs**
Stairs are the set of steps for going up or down inside a building.

stamp noun **stamps**
A stamp is a small piece of paper that you stick on an envelope or parcel before you post it.

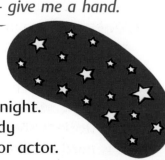

stand verb **stands, standing, stood**
When you stand, you are on your feet without moving.
Don't just stand there – give me a hand.

star noun **stars**
1 A star is one of the tiny, bright lights you see in the sky at night.
2 A star is also somebody famous, like a singer or actor.

a b c d e f g h i j k l m n o p q r s t u v w x y z

99

start verb **starts, starting, started**
When you start, you take the first steps in doing something. *My sister is just starting to read.*

station noun **stations**
1 A station is a place where you get petrol, or catch a train.
2 A station is also a building for the fire service or police.

stay verb **stays, staying, stayed**
1 If you stay somewhere, you do not move away from there. *Stay here – I'll be back in a minute.*
2 If you stay with someone or stay at a hotel, you spend the night there.

steady adjective **steadier, steadiest**
Something that is steady is not shaking at all. *Hold the ladder steady while I climb up.*

steal verb **steals, stealing, stole, stolen**
To steal is to take something that belongs to someone else.

steam noun
Steam is very hot water that has turned into a cloud.

steel noun
Steel is a strong metal made from iron.

steep adjective **steeper, steepest**
If a slope is steep, it is hard to climb.

stem noun **stems**
A stem is the main part of a plant above the ground. A stem holds a flower or leaf or fruit to the rest of the plant.

step noun **steps**
1 A step is the movement you make with your foot when you are walking, running, or dancing.
2 A step is also a flat place where you can put your foot when you are going up or down stairs or a ladder.

stick ❶ noun **sticks**
A stick is a long, thin piece of wood or something else.

stick ❷ verb **sticks, sticking, stuck**
1 If something sticks to something else, it becomes fixed to it. *The peanut butter is sticking to the roof of my mouth.*
2 If you stick something sharp into a thing, you push the point in.

stiff adjective **stiffer, stiffest**
Something that is stiff is not easy to bend.

still
Still means not moving at all. *Sit still while I brush your hair.*

sting ❶ noun **stings**
A sting is a sharp point with poison on it that some animals and plants have.

sting ② verb **stings, stinging, stung**
If something stings you, it hurts you with its sting. *A bee can sting you.*

stir verb **stirs, stirring, stirred**
When you stir a liquid or a soft mixture, you move it around with a spoon or a stick.

stomach noun **stomachs**
Your stomach is the part of your body where your food goes after you swallow it.

stone noun **stones**
1 A stone is a small piece of rock.
2 A stone is also the hard seed in the middle of some fruits such as cherries and plums.

stood See **stand**.
We stood at the bus stop for ages.

stop verb **stops, stopping, stopped**
1 If a person or thing stops doing something, they do not do it any more. *It stopped raining and the sun came out.*
2 If something that is moving stops, it comes to rest. *The bus stopped to let the people off.*

store verb **stores, storing, stored**
If you store something, you keep it until it is needed.

storm noun **storms**
A storm is very bad weather with strong wind and a lot of rain. There is sometimes thunder and lightning too.

story noun **stories**
A story tells you about something that has happened. Stories can be made up, or they can be about real things.

straight adjective **straighter, straightest**
Something that is straight has no bends or curves in it.

strange adjective **stranger, strangest**
If something is strange, it is not like anything you have seen or heard before. *What a strange creature you have drawn!*

straw noun **straws**
1 Straw is the dry stems of corn and wheat.
2 A straw is a very thin tube for drinking through.

stream noun **streams**
A stream is a small river.

street noun **streets**
A street is a road with houses and other buildings along each side.

strength noun
Strength is how strong someone or something is.

stretch verb **stretches, stretching, stretched**
When you stretch something, you pull it to make it longer, wider, or tighter. *The skin on a drum is stretched tight.*

strict adjective **stricter, strictest**
When someone is strict, they make people do what they say and obey the rules.

a
b
c
d
e
f
g
h
i
j
k
l
m
n
o
p
q
r
s
t
u
v
w
x
y
z

string noun
String is very thin rope.

strip noun **strips**
A strip is a long, thin piece of something.

stripe noun **stripes**
A stripe is a thin band of colour. *Tigers have stripes on their bodies.*

strong adjective **stronger, strongest**
1 Strong people or animals are healthy and can carry heavy things and work hard.
2 Something strong is hard to break or damage. *We tied the boat with a strong rope.*
3 Food or drink that is strong has a lot of flavour. *These mints are strong.*

stuck See **stick** ❷.
I stuck a cherry on top of the cake.

stung See **sting** ❷.
I've just been stung by a bee.

submarine noun **submarines**
A submarine is a ship that can travel under water as well as on the surface.

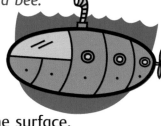

subtract verb **subtracts, subtracting, subtracted**
When you subtract, you take away.

3-2=1

suck verb **sucks, sucking, sucked**
If you suck something, you draw liquid from it into your mouth.

sudden adjective
Things that are sudden happen quickly when you do not expect them. *There was a sudden crash of thunder.*

suddenly
If something happens suddenly, it happens quickly without any warning.

sugar noun
Sugar is used to put in foods and drinks to make them taste sweet.

sum noun **sums**
A sum is a problem that you work out using numbers.

summer noun **summers**
Summer is the hottest season of the year.

sun noun
The sun gives the Earth heat and light. It is a star, and the Earth moves round it.

sung See **sing**.
I have not sung this song before.

sunk See **sink** ❷.
My boat has sunk to the bottom of the pond.

a b c d e f g h i j k l m n o p q r s t u v w x y z

sunny adjective **sunnier, sunniest**
It is a sunny day when the sun is shining.

supermarket noun **supermarkets**
A supermarket is a big shop that sells food and other things. People help themselves to things as they go round, and pay for them on the way out.

sure adjective **surer, surest**
If you are sure about something, you believe it is true or right. *I am sure I locked the door.*

surface noun **surfaces**
The surface is the outer or top part of something. *The table has a smooth and shiny surface.*

surprise noun **surprises**
A surprise is something that you did not expect. *What a lovely surprise!*

swallow verb **swallows, swallowing, swallowed**
When you swallow something, you make it go down your throat and into your stomach.

swam See **swim**.
The dog jumped into the stream and swam to the other side.

swan noun **swans**
A swan is a large, white bird with a long, curved neck. Swans live by rivers and lakes.

sweep verb **sweeps, sweeping, swept**
When you sweep, you use a broom to clear away dust and litter.

sweet adjective **sweeter, sweetest**
Sweet things have the taste of sugar.

swept See **sweep**.
Ben swept up all the leaves from the path.

swim verb **swims, swimming, swam, swum**
When you swim, you move your body through water using your arms and legs.

swing verb **swings, swinging, swung**
When something swings, it moves backwards and forwards from a fixed point.

switch noun **switches**
A switch is anything that you turn or press to start or stop something working.

sword noun **swords**
A sword is a long metal blade with a handle.

swum See **swim**.
Have you swum in the stream yet?

swung See **swing**.
The door swung open.

a b c d e f g h i j k l m n o p q r s t u v w x y z

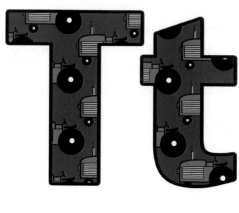

table to teach

table noun **tables**
A table is a piece of furniture. It has legs and a flat top.

tadpole noun **tadpoles**
Tadpoles are the babies of frogs and toads. Tadpoles live in water.

tail noun **tails**
An animal's tail is the part that grows out from the back end of its body.

take verb **takes, taking, took, taken**
1 When you take something, you get it in your hands. *Please take my hand while we cross the road.*
2 Take also means to bring or carry. *Don't forget to take your umbrella.*

talk verb **talks, talking, talked**
When you talk, you speak to other people. *Joe talked to Sarah on the phone.*

tall adjective **taller, tallest**
A tall person or thing measures more than usual from top to bottom.

tame adjective **tamer, tamest**
Tame animals are friendly to humans and not afraid of them.

tap noun **taps**
A tap lets you turn water on and off.

tape noun **tapes**
Some tape has a sticky back. You can use it to hold paper together.

taste ❶ noun **tastes**
The taste of something is what it is like when you eat or drink it.

taste ❷ verb **tastes, tasting, tasted**
When you taste something, you eat or drink a bit of it to see what it is like.

taught See **teach**.
My brother has been taught to swim.

tea noun **teas**
1 Tea is a hot drink, made with boiling water and the dried leaves of tea plants.
2 Tea is also a meal that people have in the afternoon or evening.

teach verb **teaches, teaching, taught**
When someone teaches, they help people to understand something, or show them how to do it. *My aunt teaches people how to paint.*

teacher noun **teachers**
A teacher is someone whose job is to teach.

team noun **teams**
A team is a group of people who work together, or who play together on the same side.

tear ❶ noun **tears**
A tear is a drop of water that falls from your eye when you cry.

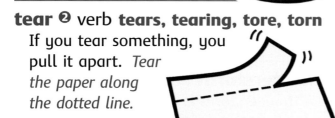

tear ❷ verb **tears, tearing, tore, torn**
If you tear something, you pull it apart. *Tear the paper along the dotted line.*

teeth See **tooth**.

telephone noun **telephones**
You use a telephone to speak to someone far away.

television noun **televisions**
A television is a machine that receives sounds and pictures through the air.

tell verb **tells, telling, told**
1 If somebody tells you something, they pass on news or information or a story. *The storyteller began to tell his tale.*
2 If someone tells you to do something, they say you must do it. *Does your dog do what you tell it to do?*

ten noun **tens**
Ten is the number **10**.

tent noun **tents**
A tent is a shelter made of strong cloth stretched over poles. People live in tents when they are camping.

term noun **terms**
A term is part of a school year. It is the time in between the holidays, when the school is open.

test noun **tests**
A test is something you do to show how much you know.

thank verb **thanks, thanking, thanked**
When you thank someone, you tell them you are grateful for something kind they have done.

theatre noun **theatres**
A theatre is a place where you go to see plays and shows.

thick adjective **thicker, thickest**
1 Something that is thick measures a lot from one side to the other.
2 Thick liquids do not flow easily.

thin adjective **thinner, thinnest**
1 A thin person or animal does not weigh very much.
2 Something that is thin does not measure much from one side to the other.

a b c d e f g h i j k l m n o p q r s t u v w x y z

105

think verb **thinks, thinking, thought**
When you think, you use your mind to work something out. *Can anyone think of the answer?*

thirsty adjective **thirstier, thirstiest**
If you are thirsty, you need a drink.

thought See **think**.
I thought I saw a cat.

thread noun **threads**
A thread is a long, thin piece of something like cotton or wool.

three noun **threes**
Three is the number 3.

threw See **throw**.
Tom threw a ball into the air.

throat noun **throats**
Your throat is the front part of your neck, and the tubes inside that take food, drink, and air into your body.

through
Through means from one side or end to the other. *We crawled through a hole in the hedge.*

throw verb **throws, throwing, threw, thrown**
When you throw something, you make it leave your hand and move through the air.

thrown See **throw**.
I've thrown my ball over the wall.

thumb noun **thumbs**
Your thumb is the short, thick finger at the side of your hand.

thunder noun
Thunder is the loud noise that follows a flash of lightning in a storm.

thunderstorm noun **thunderstorms**
A thunderstorm is a storm with thunder and lightning.

tidy adjective **tidier, tidiest**
If something is tidy, everything is in the right place and it is not in a mess.

tie ❶ noun **ties**
1 A tie is a long strip of material that is worn around the collar of a shirt and hangs down the front.

2 When two people do as well as each other in a race or have the same score in a game, it is called a tie.

tie ❷ verb **ties, tying, tied**
When you tie something, you make a knot.

tiger noun **tigers**

A tiger is a big wild cat found in India and China. It has orange fur with black stripes.

tight adjective **tighter, tightest**
If something is tight, it fits closely or is fixed firmly. *These shoes are too tight.*

time noun
1 Time is measured in minutes, hours, days, and years.
2 The time is a particular moment in the day. *What's the time?*

tin noun **tins**
You can buy food in round metal tins.

tiny adjective **tinier, tiniest**
Tiny things are very small.

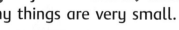

tired adjective
When you are tired, you need to rest or sleep.

today
Today means on this day. *Today is my birthday.*

toe noun **toes**
Your toe is one of the five parts at the end of your foot.

told See **tell**.
We told each other ghost stories.

tomorrow
Tomorrow means on the day after today. *See you tomorrow.*

tongue noun **tongues**
Your tongue is the long, soft, pink part that you move inside your mouth.

tonight
Tonight means the night at the end of today. *We are going to watch the fireworks display tonight.*

took See **take**.
It was lucky I took an umbrella.

tool noun **tools**
A tool is something that you use in your hand to help you do a job. Hammers and saws are tools.

tooth noun **teeth**
A tooth is one of the hard, white parts in your mouth.

top noun **tops**
1 The top of something is the highest part. *We climbed to the top of the hill.*
2 The top is the part that covers something like a jar, tube, or pen.

a b c d e f g h i j k l m n o p q r s **t** u v w x y z

a
b
c
d
e
f
g
h
i
j
k
l
m
n
o
p
q
r
s
t
u
v
w
x
y
z

tore See **tear ❷**.
Yasmin tore out a sheet of paper.

touch verb **touches, touching, touched**
1 If you touch something, you put your hand or fingers on it.
2 If things are touching, they are so close there is no space between them.

towel noun **towels**
A towel is a piece of cloth to dry yourself with.

town noun **towns**
A town is a place with a lot of houses, shops, and other buildings.

toy noun **toys**
A toy is something you play with.

tractor noun **tractors**
A tractor is a vehicle with a strong engine used for pulling heavy things on a farm.

traffic noun
Traffic is all the cars, buses, lorries, and other things travelling on the road.

train ❶ noun **trains**
A train carries people or things on railway lines.

train ❷ verb **trains, training, trained**
To train means to teach a person or animal how to do something. *I'm training my dog to walk on a lead.*

travel verb **travels, travelling, travelled**
When you travel, you go on a journey.

tree noun **trees**
A tree is any tall plant with leaves, branches, and a thick stem of wood, called a trunk.

triangle noun **triangles**
A triangle is a shape with three straight sides and three points.

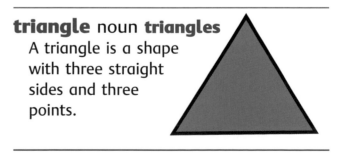

trousers noun
Trousers cover each leg and the lower part of your body.

truck noun **trucks**
A truck is a kind of large vehicle that is used to carry things from place to place.

true adjective **truer, truest**
1 If a story is true, it really happened.
2 Something that is true is right. *Is it true that a whale is a mammal?*

trunk noun **trunks**
1 A trunk is the thick, woody stem of a tree.
2 An elephant's trunk is its long nose.

try verb **tries, trying, tried**
If you try to do something, you see if you can do it. *Raj is trying to climb that tree.*

tube noun **tubes**
1 Tubes are used to hold soft mixtures such as toothpaste.
2 A tube is also a kind of pipe.

tunnel noun **tunnels**
A tunnel is a long hole under the ground or through a hill.

turn ❶ verb **turns, turning, turned**
1 When you turn, you move round or change direction. *Please turn and face this way.*
2 When something turns into something else, it changes. *A caterpillar turns into a butterfly.*

turn ❷ noun **turns**
If it is your turn, it is time for you to do something. *It's my turn to roll the dice.*

tusk noun **tusks**
A tusk is one of the two long, pointed teeth that elephants have next to their trunk.

twelve noun **twelves**
Twelve is the number **12**.

twin noun **twins**
Twins are two children who have the same parents and were born at the same time.

twist verb **twists, twisting, twisted**
1 When you twist something, you turn or bend it. *My mum twisted her ankle running for the bus.*
2 To twist also means to wrap things around each other. *Rope is made by twisting long threads together.*

two noun **twos**
Two is the number **2**.

tyre noun **tyres**
A tyre is a circle of rubber that goes round the edge of a wheel.

a
b
c
d
e
f
g
h
i
j
k
l
m
n
o
p
q
r
s
t
u
v
w
x
y
z

a
b
c
d
e
f
g
h
i
j
k
l
m
n
o
p
q
r
s
t
u
v
w
x
y
z

ugly adjective **uglier, ugliest**
People and things that are ugly are not nice to look at.

umbrella noun **umbrellas**
An umbrella is cloth stretched over a frame, which you hold over your head to keep off the rain.

uncle noun **uncles**
Your uncle is the brother of your mother or father, or the husband of your aunt.

under
Under means below. *The road went under the bridge.*

understand verb **understands, understanding, understood**
If you understand something, you know what it means or how it works.

understood See **understand**.
At last Harry understood how to do the puzzle.

undress verb **undresses, undressing, undressed**
When you undress, you take your clothes off.

uniform noun **uniforms**
A uniform is a special set of clothes people wear to show which school they go to or what job they do.

until
Until means up to a certain time. *You can stay until 4 o'clock.*

upset adjective
When you are upset, you feel unhappy and sad.

upside down
When something is upside down, the bottom part is at the top. *You're holding the picture upside down.*

urgent adjective
Something urgent is very important and you need to act quickly.

use verb **uses, using, used**
When you use something, you do a job with it. *You'll have to use a screwdriver.*

useful adjective
Something that is useful can be used to help you in some way.

usual adjective
Something that is usual is what happens most times. *We'll have dinner at the usual time.*

Vv

valley noun **valleys**

A valley is the low land between hills or mountains.

valuable adjective

Valuable things are worth a lot of money.

van noun **vans**

A van is a covered vehicle for carrying things and people.

vase noun **vases**

A vase is a pot for holding flowers.

vegetable noun **vegetables**

A vegetable is part of a plant that is used as food.

vehicle noun **vehicles**

A vehicle is anything that takes people and things from place to place. Cars, trucks, and bicycles are vehicles.

vet noun **vets**

A vet is a person whose job is to take care of sick animals.

village noun **villages**

A village is a group of houses together with other buildings in the country. A village is smaller than a town.

visit verb **visits, visiting, visited**

When you visit someone, you go to see them.

voice noun **voices**

Your voice is the sound you make when you are speaking or singing.

volcano noun **volcanoes**

A volcano is a mountain that sometimes has hot, melted rock, gases, and ash bursting out of it.

a b c d e f g h i j k l m n o p q r s t u v w x y z

wait verb **waits, waiting, waited**
If you wait, you stay for something that you are expecting to happen. *We stood waiting for the bus to come.*

wake verb **wakes, waking, woke, woken**
When you wake up, you stop sleeping.

walk verb **walks, walking, walked**
When you walk, you move along by putting one foot in front of the other.

wall noun **walls**
1 A wall is any one of the sides of a building or room.
2 Walls made of brick or stone are also used round fields and gardens.

want verb **wants, wanting, wanted**
When you want something, you feel that you would like it. *What do you want for your birthday?*

warm adjective **warmer, warmest**
If something is warm, it feels quite hot but not too hot.

warn verb **warns, warning, warned**
If you warn someone, you tell them that there is danger.

wash verb **washes, washing, washed**
When you wash, you make something clean with water and soap. *Josh needs to wash his face.*

wasp noun **wasps**
A wasp is a flying insect with black and yellow stripes. It has a sting.

waste ❶ verb **wastes, wasting, wasted**
If you waste something, you use more of it than you need.

waste ❷ noun
Waste is things that are to be thrown away, usually because the useful part has been removed.

watch ❶ verb **watches, watching, watched**
If you watch something, you look to see what happens. *Claire and Will are watching cartoons.*

watch ❷ noun **watches**
A watch is a small clock that you wear on your wrist.

112

water noun

Water is the liquid in rivers and seas. It falls from the sky as rain.

wave ❶ verb **waves, waving, waved**

If you wave, you move your hand about in the air. *We all waved goodbye as Auntie Alison drove off.*

wave ❷ noun **waves**

A wave is a moving line of water on the surface of the sea. *The waves were crashing on to the beach.*

wax noun

Wax is used to make candles, crayons, and polish. It is soft and melts easily. Some wax is made by bees, and some is made from oil.

way noun **ways**

1 The way to a place is how to get there. *Kirsty doesn't know which way to go.*
2 The way to do something is how to do it. *This is the way to hold a cricket bat.*

weak adjective **weaker, weakest**

People or things that are weak are not strong.

wear verb **wears, wearing, wore, worn**

1 When you wear something, you are dressed in it.
2 If something wears out, it becomes weak and useless because it has been used too much.

weather noun

The weather is how it is outside, for example sunny or raining.

web noun **webs**

A web is the same as a cobweb.

week noun **weeks**

A week is seven days. There are 52 weeks in a year.

weigh verb **weighs, weighing, weighed**

When you weigh something, you find out how heavy it is.

a b c d e f g h i j k l m n o p q r s t u v w x y z

113

well ❶ adjective **better, best**
If you are well, you are healthy.

well ❷
If you do something well, you are good at it, or make a good job of it.

went See **go**.
We went to Spain last year.

west noun
West is the direction you look in to see the sun go down in the evening. **W** is west.

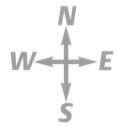

wet adjective **wetter, wettest**
If something is wet, it is covered in water, or has water in it.

whale noun **whales**
A whale is a very large sea animal. It breathes through a hole in the top of its head.

wheat noun
Wheat is a plant grown by farmers. Its seed is used for making flour.

wheel noun **wheels**
Wheels are round and they turn. Cars and bicycles move along on wheels.

wheelchair noun **wheelchairs**
A wheelchair is a chair that moves on wheels. It is used by people who cannot walk.

whisper verb **whispers, whispering, whispered**
When you whisper, you speak very softly.

whistle ❶ verb **whistles, whistling, whistled**
When you whistle, you make a loud, high sound by blowing air through your lips.

whistle ❷ noun **whistles**
A whistle is a small tube that makes a loud, high sound when you blow it.

whole adjective
Whole means all of something, with nothing missing. *She read the whole book in one go.*

wide adjective **wider, widest**
Something that is wide measures a lot from side to side.

a
b
c
d
e
f
g
h
i
j
k
l
m
n
o
p
q
r
s
t
u
v
w
x
y
z

wild adjective **wilder, wildest**
Wild animals and plants live and grow
without people looking after them.

win verb **wins, winning, won**
When you win, you beat everybody else
in a game or race.

wind noun **winds**
Wind is air moving along quickly.

window noun **windows**
A window is an opening in the wall of
a building, or in a vehicle. Windows are
for letting in light and air. Most windows
have glass in them.

wing noun **wings**
A wing is one
of the parts
of a bird
or insect that it uses
for flying. An aeroplane also has wings.

winter noun **winters**
Winter is the coldest part of the year.

wire noun **wires**
A wire is a long strip of thin metal that
can be bent easily.

wish verb **wishes, wishing, wished**
When you wish, you say or think what
you would like to happen. *I wish
I could have a puppy.*

witch noun **witches**
In stories, a witch
is a woman who
can do magic.

wizard noun
wizards
In stories, a
wizard is a man
who can do magic.

woke See **wake**.
I woke up as soon as it was light.

woken See **wake**.
Has she woken up yet?

woman noun **women**
A woman is a fully grown female person.

won See **win**.
I've won the game!

wood noun **woods**
1 Wood is the hard material that comes
from trees. It can be used to make
things like furniture and paper.
2 A wood is a lot of trees growing together.

wool noun
Wool is the thick, soft hair that covers
sheep. It is spun into thread and used
for making clothes.

word noun **words**
Words are what you use when you
speak or write. Words that are written
have a space on each side of them.

a
b
c
d
e
f
g
h
i
j
k
l
m
n
o
p
q
r
s
t
u
v
w
x
y
z

wore See **wear**.
I wore my blue jumper yesterday.

work noun
Work is a job or something that you have to do.

world noun
worlds
The world is the Earth and everything on it.

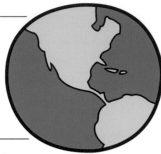

worm noun **worms**
A worm is a small animal with a long, thin body and no legs. Worms live in the ground.

worn See **wear**.
My jeans are old and worn out.

worry verb **worries, worrying, worried**
When you worry, you keep thinking about something bad that might happen.

worse
Worse means not as good as. *Your singing is even worse than mine.*

worst
Worst means so bad that none of the others are as bad as that.

worth
If something is worth an amount of money, that is how much it could be sold for. *This old watch is worth a lot of money.*

wrap verb **wraps, wrapping, wrapped**
When you wrap something, you cover it in something like paper or cloth.

wrist noun **wrists**
Your wrist is the thin part of your arm where it joins your hand.

write verb **writes, writing, wrote, written**
When you write, you put words on paper so that people can read them.
Faye is writing a letter to her uncle.

written See **write**.
She has written lots of stories.

wrong adjective
Something that is wrong is not right.
You've got the last question wrong.

wrote See **write**.
I wrote a letter to Grandma yesterday.

116

X-ray noun **X-rays**
An X-ray is a special photograph that shows the inside of a body.

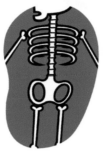

yacht noun **yachts**
A yacht is a boat with sails.

yawn verb **yawns, yawning, yawned**
When you yawn, you open your mouth wide and take a deep breath. You yawn when you are tired or bored.

year noun **years**
A year is a measure of time. There are twelve months in a year.

yesterday
Yesterday means on the day before today. *It was my birthday yesterday.*

yogurt noun **yogurts**
Yogurt or yoghurt is a food made from milk. It tastes a little sour and often has fruit in it.

young adjective **younger, youngest**
A person or animal that is young was born not long ago.

zebra noun **zebras**
A zebra is an animal that looks like a horse with black and white stripes. Zebras live in Africa.

zip noun **zips**
A zip is used to fasten two edges of material together. Some dresses, trousers, and bags have zips.

zoo noun **zoos**
A zoo is a place where different kinds of wild animal are kept so that people can go and look at them.

a b c d e f g h i j k l m n o p q r s t u v w x y z

SPELLING SUCCESS

Adding 'e' can change some words into different words. When we add 'e', it makes the vowel say its name, and not the sound that the letter makes.

Can you think of any other words like this?

tap 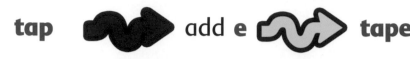 add e tape

cod  add e code

cub  add e cube

pip 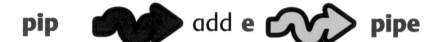 add e pipe

PUNCTUATION
Full Stops . and Question Marks ?

We use capital letters at the beginning of sentences and full stops at the end.

The special kind of full stop at the end of a question is called a question mark.

Look at the sentence and the question.

How many differences can you find?

It is playtime.

Is it playtime?

QUESTIONS
Wh- words

Why do you think these questions words are called wh- words?

Where can I play?

Which toys are mine?

When is it playtime?

Who can I play with?

What can I play with?

MAKING SENTENCES

Nouns

Nouns are naming words.

Every sentence must have a verb. Most sentences have nouns.

Verbs

Verbs are things that you are doing, having, or being.

Cheetahs run fast.   **Cheetahs run fast.**

The boy is jumping.   **The boy is jumping.**

Ahmed has black hair.   **Ahmed has black hair.**

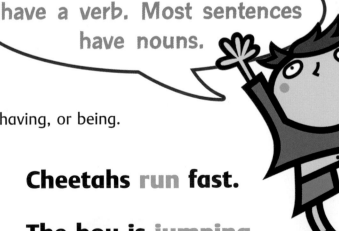

WORDS WE USE TOO MUCH

We can make writing more interesting by choosing words carefully.

Instead of writing '**said**', you could write:

shouted

yelled

cried

whispered

Instead of writing '**went**', you could write:

walked

ran

jumped

marched

Instead of writing '**nice**', you could write:

kind

happy

friendly

pretty

Instead of writing '**big**', you could write:

enormous

huge

tall

large

Can you think of sentences using each of these interesting words?

OPPOSITES

top

bottom

long

short

heavy

light

come

go

full

empty

loud

quiet

clean

dirty

fast

slow

most

fewest

Antonym is another word for 'opposite'.

PLACE AND POSITION WORDS

in

out

high

low

on

off

in front

behind

far

above

below

through

near

between

MORE THAN ONE

Look at the different ways of saying more than one.

Do you know how to say more than one child?

chick

chicks

dog

dogs

giraffe

giraffes

shark

sharks

mouse

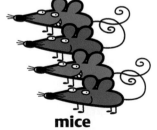

mice

goose

geese

sheep

sheep

fish

fish

123

NUMBERS

1 one   **5** five

2 two   **6** six

3 three   **7** seven   **9** nine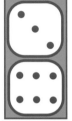

4 four   **8** eight   **10** ten

How high can you count? Which numbers do you recognise?

Ordinal numbers

1st
first

2nd
second

3rd
third

4th
fourth

5th
fifth

last

TIME

Can you tell the time on different kinds of clocks?

9:00   **12:30**   **1:45**   **3:15**

DAYS

Monday   **Tuesday**   **Wednesday**   **Thursday**   **Friday**   **Saturday**   **Sunday**

MONTHS AND SEASONS

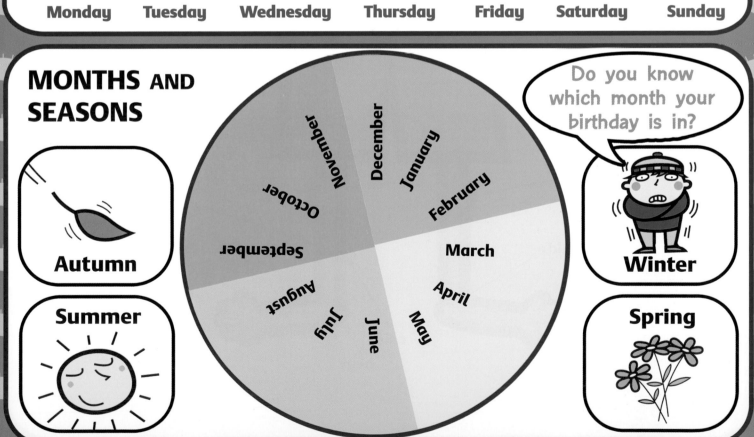

Do you know which month your birthday is in?

Autumn

Summer

November   December   January   October   February   September   March   August   April   July   June   May

Winter

Spring

125

YOUR BODY

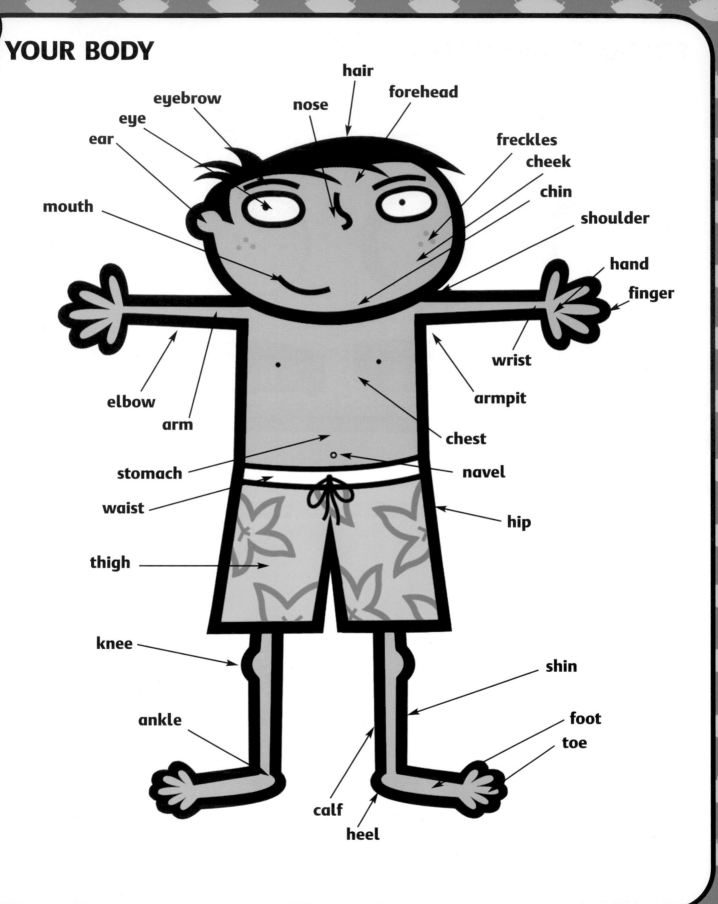

hair

eyebrow

eye

ear

nose

forehead

freckles

cheek

chin

shoulder

mouth

hand

finger

wrist

armpit

elbow

arm

chest

stomach

navel

waist

hip

thigh

knee

shin

ankle

foot

toe

calf

heel

COLOURS AND SHAPES

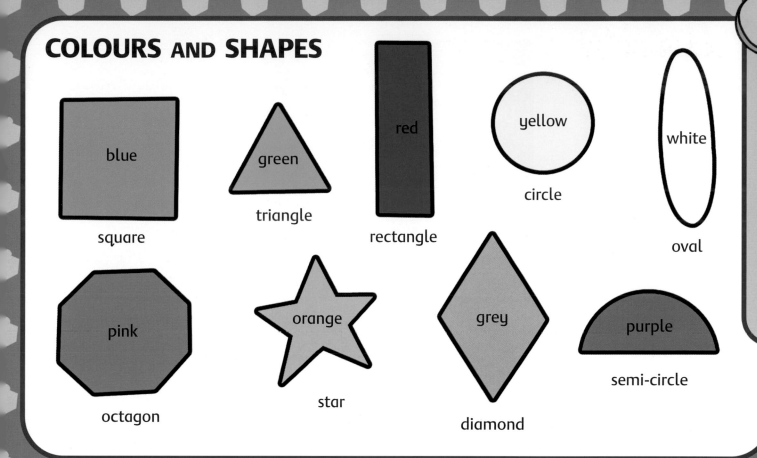

blue — square

green — triangle

red — rectangle

yellow — circle

white — oval

pink — octagon

orange — star

grey — diamond

purple — semi-circle

WORDS WE USE A LOT

a	brother	down	he	last	once	the	way
about	but	every	her	lot	only	their	we
after	by	everyone	hers	many	or	theirs	went
again	came	first	here	may	other	them	were
all	can	for	he's	me	our	then	what
am	can't	from	him	mine	ours	there	when
an	come	get	how	more	out	these	where
and	comes	getting	I	much	outside	they	which
another	coming	go	if	mum	over	this	who
any	could	goes	I'm	must	put	those	will
anyone	dad	going	in	my	she	to	with
are	did	gone	inside	myself	should	too	won't
aren't	didn't	got	into	next	sister	took	would
as	do	had	is	no	so	up	yes
at	does	hadn't	isn't	not	some	upon	you
away	doesn't	has	it	now	take	us	your
be	doing	have	its	of	taken	very	
because	done	haven't	it's (it is)	off	than	was	
been	don't	having	just	on	that	wasn't	

Age 4+

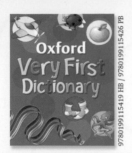 Oxford Very First Dictionary
9780199115419 HB / 9780199115426 PB

Age 5+

 Oxford First Dictionary
9780199115198 HB / 9780199115204 PB

 Oxford First Thesaurus
9780199115433 HB / 9780199115457 PB

Age 7+

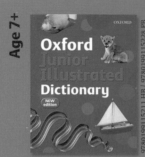 Oxford Junior Illustrated Dictionary
9780199115194 HB / 9780199115228 PB

 Oxford Junior Illustrated Thesaurus
9780199113200 PB

 Oxford Junior Dictionary
9780199113194 HB / 9780199115129 PB

 Oxford Junior Thesaurus
9780199115136 HB

Age 8+

 Oxford Primary Dictionary
9780199115334 HB

 Oxford Primary Thesaurus
9780199115167 HB

 Oxford Primary French Dictionary
9780199114931 HB / 9780199113088 PB

 Oxford Primary Spanish Dictionary
9780199115242 PB

Age 10+

 Oxford School Dictionary
9780199115341 HB

 Oxford School Thesaurus
9780199115358 HB

 Oxford School Dictionary & Thesaurus
9780199115365 HB / 9780199115372 PB

 Oxford Pocket School Dictionary
9780199115389 PB

 Oxford Pocket School Thesaurus
9780199115396 PB

 Oxford Mini School Dictionary
9780199115174 PB

 Oxford Mini School Thesaurus
9780199115181 PB

 Oxford Mini School Dictionary & Thesaurus
9780199113736 PB

 Oxford School French Dictionary
9780199115280 PB

 Oxford School Spanish Dictionary
9780199115297 PB

 Oxford School German Dictionary
9780199115303 PB

 Oxford Mini School French Dictionary
9780199115273 PB

 Oxford Mini School Spanish Dictionary
9780199115259 PB

 Oxford Mini School German Dictionary
9780199115266 PB

Age 14+

 Oxford Student's Dictionary
9780199115327 HB / 9780199115310 PB

Oxford Student's Thesaurus
9780199116522 PB

Oxford Children's Dictionaries
Think Dictionaries. Think Oxford.
www.oup.com